2nd Edition

THE STRATEGY OF PITCHING SLOW PITCH SOFTBALL

by

Michael Ivankovich

A book designed to help all Slow Pitch Softball players,
coaches, and fans in better understanding the game
of Slow Pitch Softball.

Additional copies of this book may be ordered @ 8.95 per copy from:

Diamond Press
P.O. Box 167
Maple Glen, PA 19002-0767

All questions and correspondence can be directed to the author at the above address.

Photography By
MATT PRINCE
℅ Life-Art Photos
RD 4, Box 83
Quakertown, PA 18951

Artwork By
VIRGINIA CHILDS
Cover By
JERRY DeROSA

Special Note: Wherever in this book the words "he" or "him" are used, they have been used strictly for literary convenience and are meant in their generic sense, (i.e., to include both female and male sexes).

Contents

Introduction

At one time or another, almost every young boy has aspired to become a Major League baseball player. Organized baseball competition usually starts at the Little League level and moves up one level at a time: Babe Ruth League, Connie Mack League, City Park League, Junior High School, High School Junior Varsity and Varsity, American Legion, College, etc.

Unfortunately, everyone's baseball career has to stop sometime. Injury, lack of ability, lack of interest, personal conflicts, and age are among the many reasons people stop playing baseball. Some drop out after Little League; others retire after reaching a higher level of competition. Even the fortunate few who make it to the Major Leagues reach the point where they can no longer compete. What then?

For years the answer was Fast Pitch Softball. This game requires many of the same skills as baseball: speed, agility, defense, power, base stealing, bunting, sacrificing, and strategy. The only major differences from baseball are that a bigger ball is delivered underhand on a field with shorter bases. Fast Pitch Softball has extended many players' competitive careers.

The 1940's were the golden years of Fast Pitch Softball. The level of competition was excellent and spectators were generally attracted by one person, the pitcher. The unique underhanded motion was exciting to watch and, although there were nine men on the field, winning was almost exclusively dependent upon the pitcher. If you had an excellent pitcher, you won; if not, you lost.

Initially, fans enjoyed the excitement of watching the pitcher striking out the sides and running through a line-up. However, as the years went by, pitchers became better and more dominant. They struck out so many batters that the game became boring to watch. And play.

The beginning-of-the-end to the game came when teams started stock-piling the good pitchers. A team can't win in Fast Pitch without a good pitcher and a team with a competitive schedule needs more than one pitcher. With a limited number of quality pitchers, something had to give. Those teams who attracted the good pitchers survived; those who lost their pitchers folded. The result has been a gradual decline of interest in the game of Fast Pitch Softball.

Some people say that Fast Pitch is regaining some of its earlier popularity. Others compare it to a dinosaur. Practically extinct.

Whatever the future may hold for Fast Pitch Softball, no one can deny the popularity of Slow Pitch Softball.

Slow Pitch has become the most popular form of softball in the country by far. Well over 30 million people play softball today and Slow Pitch Softball is the largest team participation sport in the country.

Why? What would make a game where the pitcher simply lobs the ball with a high arc so popular?

There are a number of reasons.

- **More people can participate.** In Fast Pitch, only nine players can play in the field. In Slow Pitch, ten players play in the field. An 11th is the extra or designated hitter (i.e., bats, but does not field). And, the re-entry rule allows a player to re-enter after leaving the game.
- **More of a team sport.** In Fast Pitch, winning is dependent upon a good pitcher. Granted, the other players must also be good athletes but, without a good pitcher, winning is very difficult. In Slow Pitch, it takes eleven people to win. Hitters can exploit a team's weaknesses easily so you need a strong defense. Scores are generally high so you need hitters who can score runs to win. And no team is totally dependent upon its pitcher.
- **There are no (or few) strikeouts.** No one likes to strike out. It's embarrassing. Humiliating. Not macho. In Fast Pitch, you can anticipate striking out each game. Not so in Slow Pitch. Rarely do you see a strike out in Slow Pitch. And when you do it usually results in some good natured teasing of the strikeout victim.
- **People of any level or ability can play.** In Fast Pitch, there is little variation in the level of competition. It's all good. Some teams are better than others, but overall there is not a wide distinction in competition. Slow Pitch, on the other hand, offers a wide variety of competition. Whatever the caliber of your team, you can find comparable competition from National Competition to local bar games: Supers, Majors, A Leagues, B Leagues,

C Leagues, D Leagues, Church Leagues, Bar Leagues, Industrial Leagues, Tournaments, pick-up games, Inter-Mural or Inter-Company Leagues, Men's Leagues, Women's Leagues.

Women? As I was growing up the worst insult a boy could face was to be accused of throwing like a girl. Girls weren't allowed to play baseball. It wasn't ladylike. They could get hurt. They shouldn't be playing sports because it wasn't nice. They should be playing with their dolls instead.

Not so today. One of the best things that has happened to Softball is the addition of women. Today girls are learning the game as early as boys. They start with tee ball and work their way up. With coaching, training, and organized competition, girls are developing their skills at a very early age.

The next 10–20 years will continue to see the continued growth of Women's Softball, especially Slow Pitch. The Women's teams that receive the most publicity today seem to be the Fast Pitch teams. They are in a comparable position to the Men's Fast Pitch teams of the 1940's. People are fascinated by one player . . . the pitcher. Spectators love watching Women's Fast Pitch games because they are amazed that a "woman" can do all those things with a softball.

The same cycle is inevitable. The best teams will gobble up the few good pitchers, leaving the remaining players with Slow Pitch Softball.

This book is intended to help everyone who plays Slow Pitch Softball better understand the game and the strategy behind it.

First, it is intended to help pitchers. To the best of my knowledge there is presently no other book devoted solely to the strategy of pitching Slow Pitch Softball. This is an undeveloped area and I hope this book will encourage other books to be written on the subject.

Second, this book will help batters better understand what they are facing in a good pitcher. If a batter understands what is going through the pitcher's mind, what he is trying to do, then the batter has a better chance of getting a hit. This may be bad for the pitcher, but it's good for the game of Softball.

Third, this book will benefit coaches because, as I said, there is no other book available on pitching. For coaches who already understand everything I say, this book should reinforce that knowledge. For those coaches who may not be entirely familiar with pitching strategies, they can read the book at home and then pretend they knew it all along.

Finally, this book will benefit the fans. Too many fans think that Slow Pitch is a simple, uncomplicated game. Pitch the ball and let the batter hit it. As the reader will see, there is much more to it than that.

This book is intended to share some insights I have developed over the past ten years. I don't profess to be a National Star. Rather, I am just one pitcher who has studied the art of pitching Slow Pitch Softball very closely. I don't expect that everyone will agree with all of my observations. I do hope that each of you learn at least a few new things. If you do, I will have succeeded in making the game of Slow Pitch Softball just a little better.

The Dream Field: Skinned infield, symmetrical fence in the outfield, regular maintenance and upkeep, even a warning track in the outfield. You probably won't play on too many fields like this.

Chapter 1

The Playing Field

The first step towards becoming an effective Slow Pitch Pitcher is to develop a clear understanding of the nature of the field you will be playing upon. It seems that practically every baseball book I have read recites the Official Rule Book when it comes to discussing the playing field. The fences should be a specified distance away, the coaches boxes should be positioned properly, the on-deck circle should be clearly lined, etc. Instructional books discuss ideal playing conditions and all pictures are taken in a neatly manicured, well-maintained professional stadium or setting.

In reality, very few Slow Pitch Softball games are played under optimum conditions. Of the 30 + million Softball players in this country, I'll bet less than 2% regularly play on officially sanctioned fields.

Actually, most Softball fields are the pits. Unless you happen to play at an especially high level of competition, or are lucky enough to play in an area backed by a supportive company or strong booster organization, most of your games are probably played on public fields. Park or school fields generally. These fields are usually poorly maintained, if maintained at all. There are probably no outfield fences, or if there are, they are an unofficial height and distance. The infield probably has bumps, ruts, and grooves. And the outfield grass needs to be cut.

There is no question that the field can have an impact on the outcome of a game. Therefore, the first step towards becoming an effective Slow Pitch Pitcher is to develop a clear understanding about the field limitations and how you can use them to your advantage.

Depending on your level of competition or the number of leagues and tournaments you play in, a typical Slow Pitch Pitcher may pitch anywhere from 15 to 150 games a year. Some of these will be on your home field, a field you should be thoroughly familiar with. Many games, however, will be played on fields you have never played on, and may never see again. Therefore, a Slow Pitch Pitcher must learn how to analyze each field he will be pitching on.

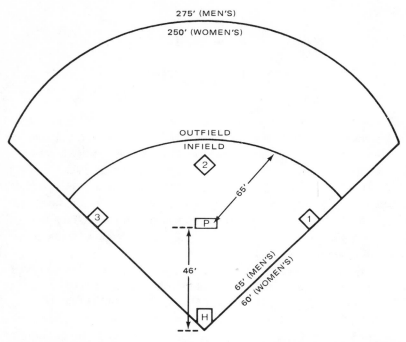

	BASES	PITCHER'S PLATE	FENCES
MEN'S	65'	46'	275' 300' (Super)
WOMEN'S	60'	46'	250'

Exhibit 1:
Key field dimensions, from the pitcher's perspective.

To begin this discussion on Slow Pitch Pitching, I have selected what I feel are a softball field's five key elements or characteristics, <u>from the pitcher's perspective.</u> These are the five areas that every pitcher should mentally note before throwing the first pitch. Each item is important and will impact either how you pitch a batter or where you position your defense.

I have broken each element into two parts. The first part is the official dimension or standard as defined by the Amateur Softball Asso-

Exhibit 1A:
Pitcher's Plate

Exhibit 1B:
Home Plate

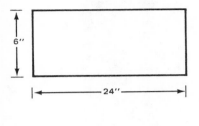

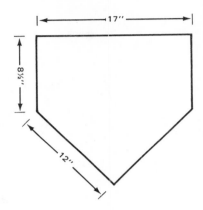

ciation.* This is what is specified in the Rule Book, both graphically and literally. These are the standards which are quoted when people discuss official dimensions and will be closely adhered to as you approach the finals in organized, sanctioned play.

The second section is what you can usually expect to find when you arrive at a field. What I call "Reality." These are the conditions you never read about in any book, but can expect to find on most softball fields, whenever you play.

1. WHAT IS THE DISTANCE OF THE BASES?

Official Dimensions:

      65' male   (exhibit 1)

      60' female (exhibit 1)

Reality: Although the basepaths for Men's Slow Pitch Softball were recently lengthened from 60' to 65', not everyone is aware of this and not all fields reflect it. It's not uncommon for the home team (or whoever brings the equipment) to simply position the bases at what appears to be the correct distance. On many fields this is the center of a wornout dirt spot that can be found near 1st, 2nd, and 3rd base. As a general rule the dirt

*The Amateur Softball Association (ASA) is an independent, national organization dedicated to developing and promoting the game of softball.

Reality: Grass (or should I say "weed") infield, unsymmetrical fences of varying distance. Dirt spots worn away 60' from home plate, little maintenance and upkeep. Most softball players are familiar with fields like this.

spots were worn out while the base rule was 60′ and this would probably indicate that the bases are incorrectly positioned.

If you are uncertain of the distance, measure it off yourself. If it is incorrect, bring it to the attention of the Umpire. 65′ bases are to the pitcher's advantage because the extra 5′ will give your infielders a little more time to cleanly field ground balls. You'll be surprised at the number of balls that at 60′ would have been clean hits, are now playable with 65′ bases.

2. WHAT IS THE DISTANCE BETWEEN HOME PLATE AND THE PITCHER'S PLATE?

Official Dimensions: 46′ from the front of the pitcher's plate to the back point on home plate. The distance is the same for both men and women. (exhibit 1)

Reality: Generally the pitcher's plate is accurately positioned, when one exists. It is not uncommon, however, for a field to be without any pitcher's plate. When this occurs, you should measure it off and clearly mark it. An experienced pitcher can feel the difference of only a few inches because he has conditioned himself to pitch from a set distance. The backswing, release, positioning of shoulders, and arc are all geared to 46′ and even a minor change can throw a pitcher off.

3. WHAT IS THE CONDITION OF THE BATTER'S BOX?

Official Dimensions: See exhibit 2 for exact dimensions

Reality: The size of the batter's box is not nearly as important to the pitcher as is the condition of it. As most batters can attest, the batter's box on many fields is badly abused and poorly maintained. Most batters have a tendency to dig a little hole with their back foot. This enables them to plant their back foot in order to obtain better leverage and a better swing. As they step into the swing, the front foot digs another little hole. The end result is that most batter's boxes are uneven.

As the season goes on, this condition becomes worse. The heat, rain, and batting practice all take their toll, especially on the right-handed batter's box since most hitters are right-handed. Even the demise of steel spikes will probably not help the situation very much. It is not uncommon for holes 3″–6″ or worse

At least this field has a pitcher's plate, right? Wrong. The pitcher's plate is only 40' from home plate, too short for Men. The Men's League must use the concrete slab as a pitcher's plate.

Most pitcher's plates are rubber and embedded in the ground. This pitcher's plate is embedded in the ground, but is actually a 2″ × 4″ piece of wood.

below home plate to appear in the place where the typical batter stands and strides. Better fields will have these holes filled periodically throughout the season. Most fields have no maintenance and this condition only gets worse.

Knowing the condition of the batter's box can impact how you pitch a batter. For example, you may find that you want to throw more short pitches than usual if you find that a batter has to step into a hole in order to reach it.

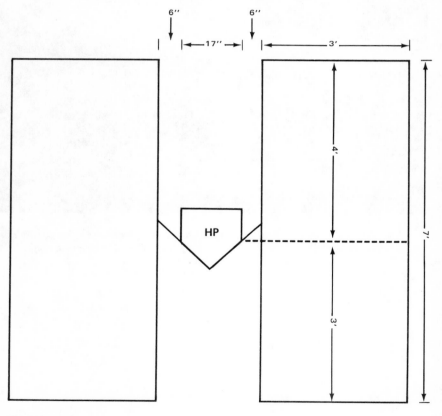

Exhibit 2:
Batter's Box

A pretty poor right-hand batter's box. Notice how much deeper the right-hand box is vs. the left-hand batter's box. Once the remaining mud is removed from the batter's box, the game will be played, and the batter's box will deteriorate even more. Even a dog walked around, rather than through, this batter's box.

4. ARE THERE FENCES IN THE OUTFIELD? IF SO, HOW FAR ARE THEY?

Official Dimension: 275' male (sometimes 300' in super competition); 250' female (exhibit 1).

Reality: Very few ballparks have fences that measure the official distance symmetrically to all fields. Most fields are open, i.e., they have no fences at all. As a pitcher, an open field is generally to your advantage. Against a weak hitting team you can position your defense as short as you feel necessary. Against a power hitting team, an open field enables you to position your outfield in such a manner that balls that would normally be home runs on a 275' fence field can still be caught for outs.

Whenever a fence exists that doesn't seem to be the official distance, measure it. Pace if off and give yourself the advantage of knowing how far the batter has to hit the ball for a home

It is very difficult for a batter to get comfortable in a deep batter's box. Notice in the picture on page 11 how a short pitch can cause the batter to swing at an uncomfortable angle. The probable result is a ball hit off-center and an out.

run. Knowing the exact distance won't prevent all home runs but it can help you decide which hitters to challenge, and which hitters to pitch around.

5. IS THE INFIELD SKINNED OR GRASS?

Official Dimension: The infield should be skinned (i.e., all grass removed). With 65′ bases, a radius of 65′ should be measured from the center of the pitcher's plate around the infield to mark the edge of the infield and the beginning of the outfield (exhibit 1).

Reality: Although they seem to be increasing in number, skinned infields are the exception rather than the rule. A skinned infield is definitely to the pitcher's advantage. The ball takes a truer hop and gets to the infielder more quickly. Although some balls may scoot through for base hits, both the infielders and pitchers appreciate the advantage of a true hop.

A grass infield, on the other hand, can cause a number of problems. Although the grass has a tendency to slow the ball, it also hides bumps and ruts. Most grass infields are poorly maintained and ground balls generally take erratic bounces. An unmowed infield only further complicates matters. Ground balls have a tendency to die in high grass so you will probably want to move your infielders in a little.

A pitcher must assess the type and condition of the infield, determine the impact it will have on ground balls, and pitch accordingly.

What I have tried to do in this first chapter is to take some relatively simple points, things that are usually taken for granted, and show you how a smart pitcher can use them to gain the upper hand. If you are one of the lucky few who regularly play on excellent fields, this chapter probably doesn't seem that important. But most softball players know what I'm talking about. If I have succeeded in whetting your appetite, we're ready for some more complex Slow Pitch pitching strategy.

In Summary:

- Few Softball fields offer ideal playing conditions.

- Few Softball fields conform to official specifications.

    Before the first pitch is thrown the pitcher should:

- Measure the distance between the bases, especially between home plate and 1st base.

- Measure the distance from home plate to the pitcher's plate.

- Assess the impact the condition of the batter's box will have on the batter's swing.

- Measure the distance of the fences if they don't appear official or symmetrical.

- Assess the impact the infield will have on ground balls.

Chapter 2

The Slow Pitch Strike Zone

The next step towards becoming an effective Slow Pitch Pitcher is to have a clear understanding of what constitutes a Slow Pitch strike. The 1987 ASA Official Softball Rule Book and Guide defines a Slow Pitch strike as follows:

> "The strike zone is that space over any part of home plate between the batter's highest shoulder and his knees when the batter assumes a natural batting stance." *

If this definition leaves you a little confused, don't worry. You're not alone. I have seen more confusion over this single point than any other aspect of the game.

Once at a tournament I was involved in a discussion with three Umpires about the definition of the Slow Pitch strike zone. Each had a different opinion of what the rule said, and meant. After 15 minutes each Umpire was still arguing about who was right.

Therefore, I'll spend this entire chapter discussing the strike zone, both according to the official rules and from my personal perspective. Before proceeding I would suggest that you read the Appendix which discusses the ASA rules that pertain to Pitching. Read it once, read it again, and then come back to this point in the book.

Now let's break the definition of a Slow Pitch Strike into several simple components. In order to be considered a Slow Pitch Strike a pitch must:

- be delivered with a perceptible arc, and reach a height of at least 6 feet (1.83m) from the ground . . . [Rule 6, Section 3c] (exhibit 3)

This rule is intended to prevent a ball from being pitched too fast. Any ball that must reach a minimum arc of 6' within a 46' distance

---

*Amateur Softball Association, 1987 Official Softball Guide and Rule Book, pg. 126, Rule 1, Section 58.

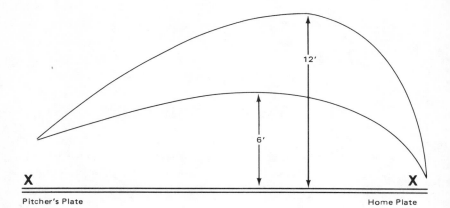

12'

6'

X   X

Pitcher's Plate   Home Plate

Exhibit 3:
Both the minimum and maximum arc are measured from the ground
to the highest point of the arc. Anything above the maximum arc or
below the minimum arc will be declared an illegal pitch and a ball will
be awarded to the batter.

obviously will not come in too fast. To further reinforce the intention
of this minimum arc rule, ASA Rule 6, Section 3a states that "The pitch
shall be released at a moderate speed." What is considered a moderate
speed is left entirely up to the Umpire's judgment.

This rule was recently changed. The previous rule was that a pitch
must have a minimum arc of 3 feet from the point where the ball was
released. This obviously was a more difficult judgment call for the umpire
so that the 6' rule has been well received by players and Umpires alike.

. . . while not exceeding a maximum height of 12 feet (3.66m)
from the ground. [Rule 6, Section 3c, (cont.)] (exhibit 3)

Like the minimum arc, the maximum arc is measured from the
ground to the highest point of the arc. Note that 12' is the present
official limit. At various times the arc restriction has varied between 10'
and an unlimited height. Some leagues still use these unofficial arc
limits.

The feeling seems to be that the unlimited arc gave good pitchers
too much of an advantage, not too unlike the pitching advantage in
Fast Pitch. Some pitchers were able to drop strikes from 20'–25' and
more, making it extremely difficult on the batter.

14

On the other hand, 10' took too much away from the pitcher, making it entirely a hitter's game. The 12' limit still keeps Slow Pitch a hitter's game, but allows smart and skillful pitchers some advantages.

- A strike is called by the Umpire for each legally pitched ball entering the strike zone before touching the ground . . . [Rule 7, Section 6a].

with the strike zone once again being defined as . . . "that space over any part of home plate between the batter's highest shoulder and his knees when the batter assumes his natural batting stance." [Rule 1, Section 58]

Wow! What does all this mean?

A Slow Pitch Strike is contrary to everything you have learned in Baseball or Fast Pitch Softball. Everyone has been taught that a strike zone is a 2-dimension target, i.e., the space above home plate between the batter's armpits and top of the knees. As shown in Chapter 1, home plate is 17" across. If we assume that an average batter has approximately 40" between the armpits and knees, we find that the average baseball or Fast Pitch strike zone is less than 5 square feet. [(17" × 40") ÷ 144" per sq. ft. = 4.72 sq. ft.].

The Slow Pitch Strike Zone is different in that it has a 3rd dimension . . . depth. In order to be a strike the pitch must cross home plate, dropping behind the batter's front knee, but in front of the back shoulder. If the pitch drops on home plate, it is a ball.

Instead of aiming at a 2 dimensional rectangle, the Slow Pitch Pitcher is really aiming at a 3 dimensional invisible cube or box. By adding the approximately 20" between the front and back shoulders, the strike zone increases from less than 5 square feet to almost 8 cubic feet. [(17" × 40" × 20") ÷ 1728 in. per cubic ft. = 7.87 cubic feet]. Any ball that crosses through that invisible box is a strike. Any pitch that misses that invisible box, falling either too short, too deep, or too wide on either side of the plate, is a ball.

It's really not as complicated as it sounds. Exhibit 4 is based on a chart found in the ASA's Umpiring Manual and I believe that it explains a Slow Pitch strike as well as can be presented.*

*Amateur Softball Association, 1984 Umpiring Manual, 9th Edition, pg. 77.

Exhibit 4:
What is a Slow Pitch Softball Strike?
Slow pitch softball strikes:
1. Must have a legal arc — minimum of six feet and a maximum of 12 feet from the ground.
2. Must be delivered at a MODERATE SPEED underhand.
3. A strike is judged when it CROSSES THE PLATE.
4. The pitched ball must pass through the strike zone which is that space over any part of home plate between the batter's highest shoulder and knees when the batter assumes a natural batting stance.

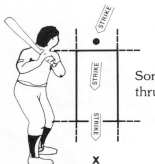

Some part of the legal pitched ball must pass thru this zone to be called a strike.

Some part of the legal pitched ball must pass thru this zone to be called a strike.

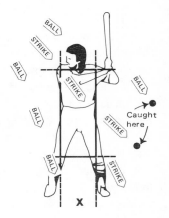

Pitches that hit the plate are ALWAYS called BALLS.

Remember that the position of the batter in the batter's box makes no difference. The plate and the batter's natural stance at the plate are the controlling factors.

This is a batter's natural stance. Shoulders relatively even, knees slightly bent, body symmetrical with home plate, waiting to swing at the pitch.

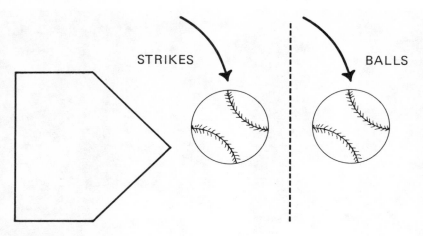

STRIKES   BALLS

Exhibit 5:
Many Umpires draw an imaginary line behind home plate to differentiate balls from strikes. You must determine where they have drawn that line.

The question of the natural stance always comes up. What does it mean? Specifically it pertains to the <u>way</u> the batter stands, not <u>where</u> he stands. A batter's natural stance is the way a normal batter stands at the plate waiting to swing. Knees slightly bent, shoulders relatively flush, waiting for the pitch. An exaggerated crouch is not a natural stance; standing on tip toes is not a natural stance. The determination of a natural stance is strictly up to the Umpire.

The position of the batter in the batter's box doesn't matter. The plate and the batter's natural stance are the sole factors in determining a strike.

In reality, the strike zone is not as precise as the technical definition would make it appear. Many Umpires seem to draw an invisible mental line somewhere behind home plate. Regardless of the arc, the key to a Slow Pitch Strike with many Umpires is <u>where the ball hits the ground</u> (exhibit 5). If the pitch drops behind home plate but in front of that invisible line, the ball is a strike. If the ball drops behind that line, the pitch is a ball. Your problem as a pitcher is to determine where that line is and then pitch to it. Chapter 9 discusses ways to determine an Umpire's definition of the strike zone.

An exaggerated crouch is not a natural stance.

Shoulders dipped, on tiptoes, is not a natural stance.

It doesn't matter where the batter stands in the batter's box. In both this picture and the picture on page 22, each of these pitches are strikes. The plate and the batter's natural stance are the controlling factors in the Slow Pitch Strike Zone.

In Summary:

- In order for a pitch to be considered a Slow Pitch strike, it:
    1. Must have an arc of between 6' and 12' from the ground.
    2. Must be delivered at a moderate speed with a perceptible arc.
    3. Must pass through an invisible, 3 dimensional box or strike zone.
    4. Cannot hit home plate.

- A strike is strictly a judgment call.

- A batter's natural stance refers to the <u>way</u> he stands, not <u>where</u> he stands.

- Only a portion of the ball must past through the strike zone, not the entire ball.

- Not all Umpires will agree on the definition of a Slow Pitch strike or call the same strike zone. Accept this as fact and learn to adjust to each particular Umpire.

- Not all pitchers will agree on the definition of the Slow Pitch strike zone either, but it's a great subject to debate over a few beers in the off-season.

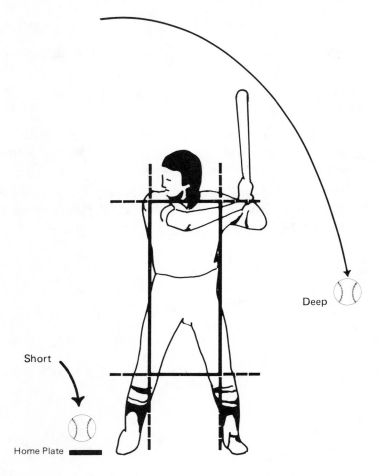

Exhibit 6:
Pitches that drop in front of the batter are not low, but "short".
Pitches that drop behind the batter are not high, but "deep".

Chapter 3

The Objectives of the Slow Pitch Pitcher

Throwing smoke, throwing BB's, throwing heat. No matter how you look at it, speed is the primary element in pitching Baseball and Fast Pitch Softball. Once your speed is sufficient to intimidate an opposing batter, you can enhance your invincibility with an assortment of curves, risers, drops, knuckles, change-ups, and the like. You fool the batter. You intimidate him. You strike him out.

How do you strike out a batter in Slow Pitch Softball? There's no speed, no intimidation. All you are doing is throwing a softball very slowly up into the air, letting the batter hit it.

How do you strike a batter out? You don't. Occasionally you may have a strike out but don't flatter yourself into thinking you did something right. You probably didn't. More than likely, it was the batter's inexperience or lack of ability that should take the credit (or blame).

From a pitcher's perspective, Slow Pitch is a game of defense, not a game of strike outs. The primary objective of any pitcher is to get the ball over the plate. Don't walk anyone unintentionally. Let the batter hit the ball so your defense can make the plays, get three outs, and go in and score some runs.

But a good pitcher takes it a step further. A good pitcher not only knows how to get the ball over the plate, he also knows how to get the batter to hit the ball where he wants it to be hit, i.e. to his defensive strengths and away from his defensive weaknesses. How do you do this? We'll get into this in Chapter 7.

First though, let's discuss some of the basic objectives in pitching Slow Pitch Softball. The most important element in pitching Slow Pitch is location. The objective of good location is to throw the batter's timing off. Location and timing then are what Slow Pitch pitching is all about.

As we have already mentioned, Baseball and Fast Pitch have a 2 dimensional strike zone: across home plate between the armpits and the knees. When throwing at this 2 dimensional strike zone, a pitcher can aim high in the strike zone, low in the strike zone, at the inside

25

corner, outside corner, or some combination of these (i.e., high and inside, etc.). Any pitch that is thrown outside the strike zone, high, low, inside, or outside, is a ball.

The Slow Pitch strike zone has the 3rd added dimension: depth. In order for a pitch to be a strike it must pass through a 3 dimensional strike zone, that invisible box across home plate between the batter's highest shoulder and his knees. The primary difference is that since we are dealing with an arc, pitches that drop in front of the invisible box or strike zone are not really low, but are "short" of the strike zone. Balls that drop behind the strike zone are not really high, but "deep". In Slow Pitch, short equals low and deep equals high (exhibit 6).

The locations that the Slow Pitch pitcher is aiming for are within the inside and outside corners, and between the front knee and rear shoulder.

Timing is probably the most important aspect of hitting. A hitter with good timing will make solid contact with the ball; a hitter without good timing will not. A baseball and Fast Pitch pitcher will try to throw off a batter's timing by varying not only the location, but the speed of his pitches. A Fast Ball and Change-Up are the two extremes but good pitchers know how to take just a little something off a pitch, slow it up just a little, to deliver a pitch that the batter doesn't expect. Getting the batter to swing just a fraction of a second early or late will cause him to swing and miss or, at the very least, will cause him to miss hitting the center of the ball.

The Slow Pitch pitcher can't use speed. Instead, he must vary the arc of the pitch to affect the batter's timing. The pitching rules state that the pitch must be between 6' and 12' from the ground. Obviously a pitch with a 6' arc will reach the plate sooner, drop slower, and drop at a different angle, than will a 12' arc. Therefore, the Slow Pitch pitcher can vary the arc in order to throw off the batter's timing.

For example, a strike can hit the exact same location in the strike zone falling at several different angles as shown in exhibit 7. Each pitch will arrive at home plate at a slightly different time, and at a different angle, than the others. The higher the arc, the closer the maximum point of the arc is to the batter.

The Slow Pitch pitcher therefore has the ability to vary not only the location of a pitch, but the height of the arc and thus the time it takes a pitch to reach home plate. Remember that none of these ele-

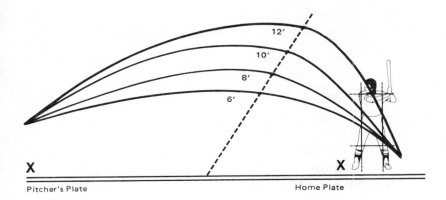

X

Pitcher's Plate   Home Plate

Exhibit 7:
The higher the arc, the closer the apex is to the batter. Note that although all 4 pitches arrive at the same point, they drop on the batter from 4 different angles.

ments is enough to strike out a batter or allow you to throw a no-hitter. But they will increase the chances of a batter making bad contact, mishitting the ball, and allowing your defense to make the play.

Let's take this a step further. You should never throw a pitch to the same location, with the same arc, two times in a row, unless you have good reason. Mix up your pitches. Short and inside, deep and outside, deep and inside. Vary the corners, vary the depth, vary the arc. Always do your best to confuse the batter. Don't let him know what is coming next. Once a batter gets a feel for you, he'll wait for the special pitch that he can pop for a home run.

Don't always throw strikes. Occasionally throw short pitches with a low arc that hit home plate. These are the best sucker pitches in the world. Flat pitches look so tempting that batters can't lay off them. A low short pitch will catch a batter over-striding and popping-up 9 out of 10 times.

Don't always throw the maximum arc. Obviously continue throwing the 12′ arc to teams that have trouble hitting it. But most good teams are used to the 12′ arc, have their timing down, and will be able to tee-off on it. Mix up your arcs, but do it wisely. Make your flatter

27

pitches tempting, balls that nibble the corners of the strike zone or, more importantly, look like they will be strikes but actually are balls.

There are several other things you should remember when considering your objectives as a pitcher:

- **You will never get everyone out.** No matter what you do, you are going to give up hits. Good hitters will get hits; bad hitters will get hits. They will get hits off of your good pitches as well as bad pitches. Slow Pitch is a hitter's game and you can never stop a team completely by yourself.

- **Prevent the long ball.** A home run can kill you. It means at least one run, more if men are on base. On the other hand, four consecutive singles means minimal damage. One, possibly two runs at the most. It is very hard and rare for a team to continue with consecutive base hits for too long. As soon as men get on base, the batter's mental state begins to change. Instead of going for a single, he begins looking for an extra base hit or a home run. He'll begin to press and will more than likely make a mistake. Anticipate it, pitch him carefully so he can't hit a long ball (i.e., don't groove it), and 95% of the time you will get him out.

- **Strive to directly cause 5–6 outs per game.** At least 50% of the outs in a game are made not because of anything the pitcher does, but because the batter makes a mistake, either mechanical or mental. Swinging at bad pitches, trying to take an outside pitch to left field, taking his eye off the ball, etc. Probably that number is closer to 75%. Exceptional defensive plays will account for 10–20% of the outs. You will usually see several diving catches or speared line drives each game.

However, a good pitcher should be directly accountable for 20–30% of the outs in any game. Getting a batter to hit into a double play in a key situation, pitching him into a position where he <u>has</u> to swing at a bad pitch to protect the plate, or setting up a batter for a sucker pitch are all ways the pitcher can directly account for outs.

In Summary

- Slow Pitch is a game of defense, not strike outs.

- Almost any pitcher can get the ball over the plate. A good pitcher has to do a great deal more than that.

- A smart pitcher gets the batter to hit to his defensive strengths, and away from his defensive weaknesses.

- A smart pitcher does not pitch to a batter's strengths; rather he pitches to a batter's weaknesses.

- The most important aspect of pitching Slow Pitch Softball is location.

- The objective of good location is to throw the batter's timing off as much as possible.

- Don't pitch to the same location two consecutive times without good reason. Vary the location and the arc.

- Expect to give up hits; try to keep runs to the minimum.

- Avoid giving up the long ball.

- Try to be directly accountable for at least 5–6 outs per game.

*In the Windmill pitching motion, the pitching arm rotates in a complete 360°
circle before releasing the ball. Few pitchers use this motion, but it is legal.*

Chapter 4

The Mechanics of Pitching

The mechanics of pitching has the tendency to be a pretty boring subject. This is intended to be a book on pitching strategy, not pitching mechanics, so I don't want to dwell on this topic too long. However, there are several points I would like to cover.

I would suggest that you return to the Appendix and read Rule 6 on pitching regulations. Again, it is very clear regarding the do's and don'ts of pitching so I won't paraphrase any of that here.

What I would like to discuss are some of the various deliveries or pitching motions that can be used. There are really 3 parts to any pitching motion:

- Grip

- Wind-up (backswing)

- Release and Follow-through

Grip

The grip on the ball depends entirely on the type of pitch being thrown. There are many different pitches that can be used. We will discuss five in the next chapter.

Wind-up (backswing)

There are several different wind-ups, or backswing motions, that can be used. The first is the Windmill. This is where, as in Fast Pitch, the pitching arm is brought out of the glove, up and around in a 360° circle prior to releasing the ball. Surprisingly, this is allowed in Slow Pitch and covered very clearly in the rules. As long as the other rules are followed, i.e. 6'–12' perceptible arc and moderate speed, the Windmill pitching motion is acceptable. Why anyone would want to use the Windmill in Slow Pitch is beyond me. The only people I have ever

In the Full Backswing, the pitching arm goes as far past the hip as possible on the backswing. Nothing awkward, just try to be as comfortable as possible.

seen use it were inexperienced novices who obviously didn't know what they were doing. I have never seen anyone use it effectively in Slow Pitch.

The second wind-up motion is called the Full Backswing. Here the pitcher swings the pitching arm back before bringing it forward for the release. Some pitchers use a Full Backswing, i.e., bringing the arm back

In the Partial Backswing, the pitcher's arm goes back approximately half as far as in the Full Backswing.

as far as possible. Others only bring the arm part of the way back. Both of these wind-ups are common and frequently interchanged in an attempt to throw off a batter's timing.

A third motion that can be effectively used is not really a wind-up at all. The pitcher begins by holding the ball in front of him. Instead of taking any backswing at all, he simply begins the forward motion with

In the No Backswing pitching motion, the ball never goes past the hip. Begin by holding it in front of you, as above. The hand will drop around 6-8" before going forward towards the release point. Notice that in this picture, as in the previous three, the pitcher's toe is on the rear of the pitcher's plate rather than the heel being positioned on the front of the pitcher's plate.

the ball in front of him and releases the ball at the appropriate point. The ball never goes back past his hip. Personally I don't feel as comfortable with this but it can be used as effectively as either the Full or Partial Backswing.

In the One Step Approach, both feet begin flat on the ground, pivot foot on the pitcher's plate, left foot behind the pitcher's plate. Near the point of release, the left foot moves one step towards home plate. (See page 36.)

Release and Follow-through

There are two distinct ways to release the ball, each of which is correct. The first is the <u>One-Step Release</u>. In this release, the pivot foot (right foot for right-handed pitchers) is positioned firmly on or touching the pitcher's plate. The left foot is either on the pitcher's plate or slightly behind it. As the arm begins to move towards the batter and the point of release, the left foot steps toward the plate. At the point of release the arm continues to follow through up as high as it will go. This follow

through will help you to achieve the maximum arc. This is the most frequently used release and seems to be comfortable for most pitchers.

The second approach is a <u>No-Step Release</u>. Here, the feet are positioned in the same manner as the One Step. However, instead of stepping towards the plate, the feet remain stationary at the point of release. The knees bend and, in effect, you bounce up as you release the ball. Once again, the arm continues up as high as possible after releasing the ball.

This release is generally used by more experienced pitchers. The advantage is that it is easier to back up several steps into a defensive posture from this release. Not only are you one step farther back at the point of release but you do not have to change from a forward to backward momentum in order to begin your back step.

In the No Step Approach, the left foot does not move forward. Instead it stays behind the pitcher's plate, even after the ball has been released.

In order to achieve the maximum arc, your pitching arm must continue to follow-through, even after the ball has been released. If you are not achieving the maximum arc, you are probably not following through completely.

Both of these releases are effective and each can be used interchangeably to throw a batter's timing off.

Pitcher's Plate

The Pitcher's plate or pitching rubber is used to clearly mark for the pitcher and the Umpire the exact spot a pitcher is supposed to pitch from. The exact distance should be 46' from the back point of home plate to the front of the pitching rubber.

Some pitchers prefer to begin with their heel on the pitcher's plate, while others begin with their toe on the back of the pitcher's plate (see photo on page 40). Notice that in all of the pictures in this chapter, the pitcher begins with his toe on the pitcher's plate. This is the preferred position of most experienced Slow Pitch Pitchers.

In baseball and Fast Pitch, the pitching rubber is also used to gain speed on the ball. It is firmly embedded in the ground and these hard-throwing pitchers will generally use their pivot foot to push off the pitching rubber, giving them added leverage and momentum in their delivery.

This is not necessary in Slow Pitch. Since there is no speed in the delivery, there is no need to push off. Some Slow Pitch Pitchers begin

with the heel of their right foot on the pitcher's plate, and the toes in front, exactly as in Fast Pitch. There is nothing wrong with this if it feels comfortable, especially if you are using the One Step release.

More experienced pitchers generally put the toes of their pivot foot on the back of the rubber, just barely touching it. The primary advantage of this is that you never have to contend with the hole in front of the rubber which has been dug by Fast Pitch Pitchers. You are also several inches farther away from the batter. Pitching can be a game of inches and you can field more balls at 46'6" than you can at 46'0".

One final point to remember is that there is no "balk" in Slow Pitch Softball. If you feel uncomfortable at anytime during your wind-up, release, or follow-through, you can stop without penalty. No base runner will advance and you can begin again.

In Summary

- Be comfortable in your delivery.

- You can vary the degree of Backswing, or not use one at all, in an attempt to throw off a batter's timing.

- The follow through after releasing the ball is necessary to achieve a maximum arc.

- Experienced pitchers pitch in a manner that will allow them to effectively back up several steps into a defensive position after releasing the ball.

- There is no balk in Slow Pitch.

Finger Roll

Reverse Finger Roll

Chapter 5

Types of Pitches

Each pitcher has his own assortment of pitches. Some are easy to master, others take years of practice. What we will discuss here are some of the more basic pitches. As you learn the easier ones, you can progress to some of the more difficult ones.

The most important thing for a beginning pitcher is to develop several pitches you feel comfortable with. My personal experience is that although I use five basic pitches, I feel more comfortable with some more than others on any given day. When I have trouble controlling one pitch, I then have others I can resort to with confidence.

Finger Roll

The most basic pitch is the Finger Roll. You simply grasp the ball with your palm facing up, thumb on the top stitch, fingers on the bottom stitch. At the point of release, the ball simply rolls off the finger tips and floats toward the plate rotating slowly with a moderate front to back spin (exhibit 8). It has a natural spin, not really enough to affect the descent towards the plate or impact the point of contact. This is simply an easy, free-flowing pitch that most pitchers begin with and feel very comfortable using.

This pitch can be thrown with a complete backswing which goes well past the hip, or it can be thrown without any backswing at all. Do what is most comfortable at first, and later, vary the length of backswing to throw the batter's timing off.

Reverse Finger Roll

The second pitch is the Reverse Finger Roll. This is almost exactly like the finger roll except the palm is facing down rather than up. The backswing can have the same variation, and again, the ball simply rolls off the fingertips and thumb and floats toward the plate. The primary difference is that the spin is reversed, this time rotating slowly with a moderate back to front spin (exhibit 9). This is also a natural spin, nothing too exaggerated or pronounced.

43

What is the effect of the change in spin? This used to be my bread and butter pitch, the one I felt most comfortable with. I used to hear opponents comment to each other: "Be careful, he has a reverse spin on the ball." I loved hearing that because that gave me the psychological edge. They were concerned about something they should not have been worried about. The reverse spin meant nothing because it was too slow to have any impact. I simply pitched that way because it felt more comfortable than the Finger Roll. However, since fewer pitchers use the Reverse Finger Roll, I stood out from other pitchers and opponents assumed I had devious intentions in pitching that way.

Floating Curve

The third pitch I use is what I call a Floating Curve. "Impossible. You can't throw a curve ball in Slow Pitch Softball," the guy said to me. He didn't believe me but I had seen it with my own eyes.

I was coaching a Women's All Star Team and the pitcher had a natural curve that floated in towards a right-handed batter a good 12"–18". I watched her again and again and it wasn't my imagination. I brought the other coach over and he couldn't believe it either. We watched her again and again until we finally learned the key.

Unlike the two Finger Roll pitches, this pitch has a different grip. The thumb grasps the lower left stitch while the index finger grasps the upper right stitch. The other fingers support the ball naturally.

This pitch is thrown with a normal backswing and then a pretty strong flick of the wrist. Similar to throwing a frisbee but not quite that

Exhibit 8:
Finger Roll. (Note forward spin)

Exhibit 9:
Reverse Finger Roll. (Note reverse spin)

Floating Curve

drastic. Also, the release is somewhat different. At the point of flicking the wrist, the thumb points to 8:00, the index finger to 2:00.

Does this pitch have the same impact as a Fast Pitch curve? No. In reality, this pitch is more like a Fast Pitch Slider in that it breaks in on a right-handed batter, and away from a left-handed batter.

Will you strike anyone out using it? No.

This pitch can give you an advantage against the batter who knows he is going to swing before the ball is pitched. A right-handed batter begins swinging at a pitch on the outside corner and ends up hitting a pitch on the inside corner (exhibit 10). The opposite is true for a left-handed batter.

This pitch will work better and float more on warm, dry days rather than on cold, damp days. The density of the air seems to affect the float. It's not the most important pitch to throw, just another in your bag of tricks.

Exhibit 10:
Birdseye view of a floating curve ball.

Knuckle Ball

The fourth pitch is a <u>Knuckle Ball</u>. The nice thing about this pitch is that the ball hardly rotates as it floats towards the plate, maybe 1 or 2 revolutions at the most. It has two primary advantages. First, it lets the batter see the stitches on the ball, think about it, become a little more anxious, and will perhaps throw his timing off. Second, it gives you the <u>image</u> in your opponent's mind of being a knowledgable pitcher, perhaps more than you deserve. But since so few pitchers throw the Knuckle Ball, you will appear to be a rare and exceptional pitcher.

You can throw this pitch in several ways. I prefer the thumb on the lower left stitch, 4th finger on the upper right stitch, and the index and middle finger up on the manufacturer's name. The backswing and release are similar to the Reverse Finger Roll.

An alternate way to throw the Knuckle Ball is with the index and middle finger on the cross stitch above the manufacturer's name. This pitch would have a backswing and release similar to the Finger Roll pitches.

Knuckle Ball, knuckles on brand name

Knuckle Ball, knuckles on cross stitch above brand name

Does the ball really move around? Rarely. Rather, it comes in dead. It just seems to float so slowly that the batter can almost count the stitches.

The one exception is when this pitch is thrown into the wind. When a dead ball is thrown into the wind, it does very funny things, just like a baseball Knuckle Ball. You don't know where it is going but the movement is so erratic the batter doesn't know either.

In one State Tournament we were facing a team far superior to us in terms of power. Most of the line-up was capable of hitting the long ball and several of them did in the 1st inning. The wind was blowing directly toward center field and therefore, directly at me. These guys hit me pretty well and I was forced to go to the Knuckle Ball early. The conditions were just right and I was able to consistently get the Knuckle Ball over the plate, although I didn't know what part of the strike zone it would hit. It moved around a lot and I even had 2 or 3 swinging strike-outs that day against good hitters. Did we win? Well . . . no. But we did hold them to no more runs the rest of the game and we lost something like 6–4.

In hindsight, I probably should have thrown the Knuckle Ball sooner.

Reverse Back Spin

The fifth pitch that I use is my favorite, and also my most effective. It is called the Reverse Back Spin. It is held in a manner similar to the Floating Curve, with the thumb on the lower left stitch. However, the index and middle finger are held on either side of the upper right stitch.

I take a normal backswing and, at the point of release, the thumb spins down while the fingers spin up. This does cause a severe backspin on the ball and gives me two primary advantages.

1. The more pronounced spin causes the ball to drop on a different angle than other pitches. The apex of the arc is closer to the plate and therefore, the ball descends at a steeper angle upon the plate, thereby impacting the batter's timing (exhibit 11).

2. The more pronounced spin on this pitch does have an effect on the batter. Balls hit dead center will travel; there's not much that can be done about it. However, balls hit off center, either above or below the sweet spot, have a greater tendency of becoming routine ground balls or pop flys.

As I said, this is my most effective pitch and the one I use 80% of the time.

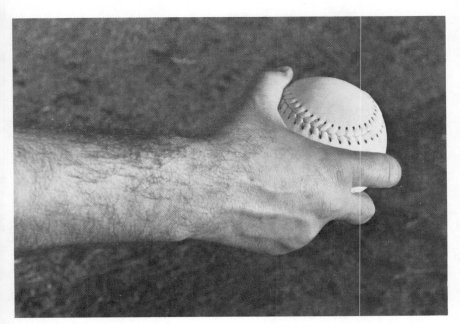

Reverse Back Spin

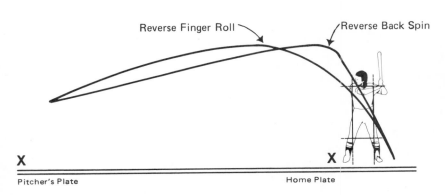

Exhibit 11:
Reverse back spin. (Note that the more dramatic spin causes it to reach its apex later, and drop at a different angle, than the reverse finger roll.

These pitches are not easy to master. They have taken years to develop and practice. I can't over emphasize the need for you to develop your own assortment of pitches. Watch other pitchers or invent your own. And practice. It will pay off in the long run.

In Summary

- It takes years of practice to develop a wide assortment of pitches.

- You should develop a wide variety of pitches and you should use the pitches you feel most comfortable with on any given day.

- The more spin on the ball, the harder it is to cleanly hit.

- The image you set in the other team's mind regarding your pitching ability can work to your advantage.

- You <u>can</u> throw a Knuckle Ball and a Curve Ball in Slow Pitch Softball.

- A wide assortment of pitches will help you in throwing a batter's timing off.

Chapter 6

Types of Softballs

Softballs, they're all round and have little stitches on them. What difference does it make which one you pitch with. They're all the same, aren't they?

Nothing could be further from the truth. At lower levels of competition, with no power hitters in the line-up, the type of ball makes little difference. But as soon as you add one or more power hitters, the type of ball becomes increasingly important. It can even make the difference between winning and losing the game.

First, let's take a look at the composition of a softball and the different types of softballs available. Later in Chapter 10 we will look at several strategies involving the softball you can use to your advantage.

Rule 3, Section 3 of the ASA Official Guide defines the required characteristics of a legal softball (see Appendix). This is a clear technical definition but let's be a little more specific. Actually all legal softballs have three distinct parts:

- Core

- Winding

- Cover

The Core is the center of the ball. It is generally made of long fibre kapok or compressed cork and is the largest part of the ball, having a diameter of approximately $3\frac{1}{2}"$.

Surrounding the Core is a relatively thin layer of thread called the Winding. This cotton/polyester thread is tightly wrapped around the core and measures about $\frac{1}{16}"$. The ball is then dipped into a special chemical solution to solidify and strengthen the winding.

Finally, the Core and Winding are surrounded by a Cover. Generally the Cover is of top grade leather, although some balls are wrapped with a synthetic leather cover. The Cover is then cemented to the Winding and hand-stitched with a nylon thread and is approximately $\frac{1}{16}"$ thick.

The 3 layers of a softball: Core, Winding, and Cover

These three physical characteristics of a softball can be varied to produce several different types of softballs. Each type has a special use or purpose within the game of Slow Pitch and every pitcher should be able to identify each ball and understand its capabilities.

Basically, softballs are manufactured to have varying resilience levels. The resilience level determines how far a ball will actually travel and is called the "Coefficient of Restitution." What this means is that, given exactly the same type of swing, and assuming that all other variables are the same, a ball with a higher Coefficient of Restitution will travel farther than a ball with a low Coefficient of Restitution.

It is imperative that the pitcher understand the differences between the various softballs because each one is capable of traveling a different distance. For our purposes, we will discuss five types of softballs.

Official Fast Pitch Softball (White Stitch): Since Fast Pitch Softball allows fewer hits than Slow Pitch, a lively ball is generally more desirable. This ball is constructed with a relatively high Coefficient of Restitution and can be identified by its white stitches. Although prescribed only for Fast Pitch, many lower level Slow Pitch Leagues use it during league play because it travels farther and allows more home runs. You may also see this ball when playing in non-sanctioned tournaments as well.

Restricted Flight (Red Stitch): At higher levels of competition, most batters in the line-up are capable of putting a white stitched ball over a 275′ fence. In order to keep the game competitive and within reason, the Restricted Flight ball was developed. This ball has a lower Coefficient of Restitution than the white stitch ball and will travel an approximately 8% shorter distance when hit. This ball can be identified by its red stitches and has been required in all sanctioned Slow Pitch tournaments.

Restricted Flight (Gold Stitch): As the quality of competition has continued to improve, the Red Stitch Restricted Flight ball has become less desirable at higher classifications of play. Even with the Red Stitch Restricted Flight ball, many batters can still routinely pop home runs over 275′ fences. For example, in the 1984 Men's Major Slow Pitch National Tournament in Garland, Texas, 808 home runs were hit over the course of one weekend!*

Obviously something had to be done. The result is the Gold Stitch Restricted Flight ball. This ball has a significantly lower Coefficient of Restitution and will travel an approximately 15% shorter distance than will the traditional White Stitch ball.

The Red Stitch ball will continue to be used in lower level sanctioned tournaments, while the Gold Stitch ball will be used in higher level sanctioned tournaments.

Maximum Distance: It had to happen. It was only a matter of time before a livelier ball was introduced. Softball players are generally macho jocks who want to hit more, not fewer, home runs. Although not allowed in sanctioned play, don't be surprised to find the ball used in lower level League play or non-sanctioned tournaments.

As the pitcher, you should always be aware when this ball is being used. You are closer to the batter and have less time to react than anyone else on the field.

Depending on the manufacturer, this ball can have blue, red, or white stitches so inspect the ball closely before pitching. This ball has a high Coefficient of Restitution and is significantly livelier than the Fast Pitch White Stitch ball or any of the other Restricted Flight balls.

Synthetic Cover: All the previously mentioned balls have top grade leather covers. Occasionally you will find a ball with a synthetic cover. The core and winding are identical to the leather covered ball

*ASA Balls & Strikes, Vol. 52, No. 8, Oct., 1984, pg. 17.

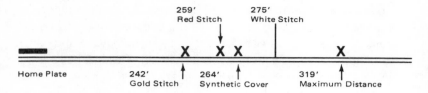

259'
Red Stitch

275'
White Stitch

X   X   X   X

Home Plate   242'   264'   319'
               Gold Stitch   Synthetic Cover   Maximum Distance

Exhibit 12:
What is a home run with a White Stitch or Maximum Distance ball is
not a home run with a Gold Stitch, Red Stitch, or Synthetic Cover ball.

but the synthetic cover itself is slightly different. The advantage of this
ball is that the synthetic cover won't pick up moisture when the ground
is wet, allowing for longer and more economical use of the ball. The
disadvantage is that the thicker cover accounts for approximately 4%
less flight than the white stitch ball.

Exhibit 12 gives a comparison between the five balls we have
discussed. For the sake of comparison, assume that an official Fast Pitch
White Stitch ball will barely clear a 275' fence for a home run. Given
the same impact and swing, and if all other variables were the same
(wind, weather, etc.), a Maximum Flight ball will clear that 275' fence
by a significant margin, while the Gold Stitch Restricted Flight, Red
Stitch Restricted Flight, and Synthetic Cover balls all fall short of the
fence.

Do you still believe that all softballs are the same?

In Summary

- Not all softballs are the same

- You can generally determine the type of ball by the color of its
  stitches.

- White Stitch and Blue Stitch balls will generally travel the farthest.

- Red Stitch balls are Restricted Flight.

- Gold Stitch balls are also Restricted Flight and will travel a shorter
  distance than any other ball.

- A Maximum Flight ball has recently been introduced into the
  market but is not prescribed for use in sanctioned games.

Chapter 7

Analyzing a Batter's Weaknesses

This is probably the most important chapter in the book. The first six chapters discussed the "how to's" of pitching. We have looked at the strike zone, the pitcher's objectives, the mechanics of pitching, five different pitches, and five different types of softballs. Mastering these things alone will take years of practice.

But mastering the art of location is not enough. Being able to pitch to a precise location doesn't in itself make you a good pitcher. The most important part of pitching is knowing *when* to pitch to a precise location. A top notch pitcher knows how to analyze a batter's style and identify his weaknesses almost instantaneously. Once the pitcher has identified the batter's weakness, he can then pitch to that weakness and exploit it to its fullest advantage.

Let's begin with the premise that every batter has at least one weakness. That weakness may be technical, i.e., how he stands, holds the bat, swings, etc. Or, that weakness may be mental. He may think he is a home run hitter when he is not, he may be too proud to take a walk, or, without realizing it, he may signal his intentions to you by the way he stands or by the direction he looks with his eyes. I have never seen a batter who can consistently hit 1.000. Most don't even hit .500. Therefore you can assume that all batters have at least one weakness. Your objective as a pitcher is to locate that weakness and exploit it.

I utilize a 4-step approach in observing a team and analyzing its weaknesses. Each step has a purpose and will provide you with a little information about the batters you will be facing.

The first step is to observe the opposing team before their batting practice even begins. Watch them as they arrive at the field and as they loosen up. You will be surprised at what you can learn. Specifically, look for four things:

- **Size:** How big are they? If they are all big musclemen, you could be in trouble. They could be a bunch of home run hitters. On the other hand, they could be a team of head jobs who hit long outs. Are they small? They could be a group of inexperienced kids. Or, they could be a fast, line-drive hitting team who hit the ball and run to second base. As a general rule, a team's size will determine where you position your outfield in the early innings until you get a better feel for their strengths and abilities.

- **Ability:** Watch them loosening up on the side lines. Do they warm up like experienced ball players? Do they have good arms? Do they loosen up and exercise before throwing? Do they look like they know what they are doing? Or do they appear to have weak arms, little experience, and an overall lack of ability.

- **Equipment:** Observe their equipment. Do they have top quality softball gloves or small baseball gloves? Does each player bring his own bat? Does the team have current model bats in their bat bag or are they using bats from 4-5 years ago?

  Don't let uniforms fool you. Any team with a good sponsor or booster organization can have uniforms. Uniforms are generally a sign of good organization, not ability.

  However, there is a direct correlation between what a player spends out of his own pocket and ability. You will find that better softball players will generally spend more on equipment than will inexperienced ballplayers. Therefore, the more personal equipment a team brings, the more experience they probably will have.

- **Leaders:** Keep your eye on those players who appear to be team leaders. A team leader is not generally the nicest guy but the best all-around ballplayer. He is the guy who probably makes the big plays for his team and who you may have to face in an important situation. Learn to recognize the team leaders early so that they don't surprise you late in the game.

After you have formulated some general impressions about your opponents, the second step in analyzing a team's weaknesses is to observe their batting practice. Batting practice can give you additional knowledge about the opposing team in general. If the batting practice is organized and well run, it can be an indication that you are playing against a serious, disciplined team. If the batting practice is poorly run, disorganized, and a waste of time, you are probably playing a team of jokers.

Specifically look for two things during batting practice. First, are there any areas left unattended, e.g. right field. If no one is standing in right field, that probably tells you that they have no opposite field hitters, or if fielders move into an unattended area for only one or two hitters, that is an indication that those hitters are capable of doing things that others on the team are not.

Secondly, watch how the batting practice pitcher pitches. If he consistently uses a high arc or varies his pitches, it will be an indication that they are used to dealing with better pitching. On the other hand, all flat pitches during batting practice could mean they will have trouble with a 12' arc.

Batting practice will also give you the opportunity to observe individual batters for the first time. Try to watch each batter and make mental notes, looking for the following points:

- Is he big or small?

- Is he athletic looking?

- Does he appear fast or slow?

- Is he a long ball hitter or a singles hitter?

- Is he capable of hitting a ball through an outfield gap?

- Does he hit to all fields or does he only hit to one field?

- Did the outfield move out or move in when he came to bat?

- Do his team mates show him respect?

Remember that although these initial observations don't tell you everything about a batter or a team, they will give you some preliminary indications of what you are up against. Batting practice is an excellent place to begin looking for technical and mechanical weaknesses and, as a pitcher, you should spend as much time as possible before a game observing the opposing team.

The third step in analyzing individual batters is to observe where they bat in the line-up. Overall, teams construct their line-ups in a very similar manner and generally you can break the line-up into five distinct groupings. Batters within each group generally share some similar characteristics.

Batter	General Characteristics
1, 2	fastest players on the team; able to get on base consistently; smart enough to take walks; frequently make it to second base.
3, 4, 5	best power; most consistent power; proven hitters; generally free swingers; take relatively few walks.
6, 7	some power; not as consistent as #3–5.
8, 9, 10	weaker hitters than #1–7; generally slower; less power; less consistent hitters.
11	- on weaker teams, the slowest, weakest batter on the team. - on smarter teams, the #11 batter is usually stronger than the #10 batter. With the number of at bats virtually the same, it is not desirable to have the slowest runner preceding the fastest runner (#1 batter).

Up to this point your analysis has been taking place prior to game time. The fourth and final step in analyzing a batter's weaknesses occurs once the game has started. This is the most important step because now it's you vs. the batter. You've watched him in batting practice, you know where he bats in the line-up, but this is the real thing. If you are correct in your analysis, you stand a good chance of getting him out. If you are wrong, he stands a good chance of getting a hit.

Exhibit 13 covers some of the things you should observe when the batter is standing at the plate. Watch the batter closely, looking for some indication of weakness or, better yet, his intentions. The batter's stance, grip, stride, and location he is aiming for should be considered before pitching.

For example, if the batter has an exaggerated crouch, pitch him deep and tight. From a crouch he will most likely get under the pitch and pop it up. It is very hard to hit a ground ball on a deep pitch without "tomahawking" the ball.

Exhibit 13

ANALYZING BATTING
CHARACTERISTICS & WEAKNESSES

Things to look for:	Recommended pitch:
Stance	
1) erect	short
2) crouch	deep
3) crowds plate and looking towards the opposite field	inside and deep
4) crowds plate and looking to pull	outside and deep
5) stands away from plate and looking towards the opposite field	inside and deep
6) stands away from plate and looking to pull	outside and deep
Grip on bat	
1) choked up	deep
2) normal grip at end of bat	short
Type of hitter	
1) pull hitter	outside
2) opposite field hitter	inside
Stride	
1) steps toward plate	tight, on the hands
2) steps away from plate	outside and short
3) long stride (overstriding)	deep and tight or deep and away
4) bucket stepper	short and away or deep and away
Miscellaneous	
1) rear shoulder drops	deep and tight
2) hand hitch	deep and tight

EXHIBIT 14

TEAM:_____   DATE:_____

	name	BATTER
	uniform #	
	batting order #	
	erect	STANCE
	crouch	
	away from plate	
	crowds plate	
	regular	GRIP
	choke	
	pull	TYPE OF HITTER
	straight away	
	opposite field	
	spray	
	long ball	
	good bat control	
	towards plate	STRIDE
	away from plate	
	long stride	
	bucket stepper	
	misc.	
	drops shoulder	MISC.
	hand hitch	
	swings at 1st pitch	
	doesn't take walk	
	doesn't go to 2 strikes	
		COMMENTS

If the batter is a pull hitter, pitch outside. It is very difficult to effectively pull an outside pitch. The result is usually a ball hit off center and an out.

Sometimes it may be necessary to trick the batter into signaling his intentions. If you feel he wants to go to right field, throw him an intentional ball just outside the strike zone. A body motion or movement of the feet could give his intentions away. Once you know the batter's intentions, you can pitch accordingly.

For those of you who are so inclined, the chart in exhibit 14 can be used in scouting an opposing team. It can be used during their batting practice, or perhaps when you are watching them in action against another team.

I can't overemphasize the importance of learning how to analyze an opposing team. The better you become at spotting a weakness, any weakness, the greater your chances of getting a batter out. You will never be able to get everyone out all the time. But, the more you know about an opposing team and the individuals on it, the better your chances are of winning.

In Summary

- All batters have at least one weakness. Your objective is to locate that weakness and exploit it.

- Uniforms are usually a sign of good organization or a strong booster organization, not of a team's ability.

- There is generally a direct correlation between what a player spends on equipment out of his own pocket and his overall ability.

- You can learn a lot about a team by watching their batting practice.

- A batter's position in the line-up can give you an indication of his strengths and ability.

- A smart team will position their weakest, slowest hitter #10 instead of #11 because there is less likelihood he will slow up the #1 hitter, should he get on base.

- The most important analysis you make of a batter's weakness is the one you make during the game.

- You can sometimes trick a batter into giving his intentions away.

- The better you become at spotting a batter's weaknesses, the greater your chances of winning.

Chapter 8

Defense at the Pitching Position

Slow Pitch is a hitter's game. That's why there are ten fielders instead of nine. That's right, ten fielders. A pitcher's job isn't over after releasing the ball. As soon as the ball is released the pitcher has to change his mindset from "How do I pitch this batter" to "What do I do when the ball is hit to me."

The pitcher is closer to the batter than any other defensive player. Only 46' away. Less if he uses the One-Step Approach and doesn't back up.

One of the primary reasons the pitcher has to play defense is protection. Self-preservation. You have less time to react than anyone else. If you are not concentrating every second, you run the risk of being hit by a line-drive or ground ball, causing serious injury to yourself.

Some batters are soft-hearted souls who wouldn't want to hurt a fly. They realize that the pitcher is very close and could get hurt. They purposely hit the ball away from the pitcher so they won't have his injury on their conscience.

Most softball players have no conscience. They feel that softball season is open hunting season on the pitcher. After you have lobbed the ball up, the batter has time to watch it and think about where to hit it. To your right, to your left, at your feet, or at your head. Never lose sight of the fact that you have less time to react than any other fielder. Always assume that each batter is aiming for your head and be ready for it.

From a more strategic point of view, a pitcher needs to play defense in order to block-up the middle. There is a big gap between the short-stop and 2nd baseman and a pitcher who cannot play defense gives the batter a large target to aim for. Exhibit 15 gives you an idea of the gap up the middle using a 4-across defense. Anything that gets by the pitcher is at least a single, more if it gets between the left-center fielder and right-center fielder.

On the other hand, if the pitcher is a good defensive player and can block the middle, you will have gained a psychological edge over your opponents. If they feel that they can't get the ball by you, they either have to try to hit it into another gap or over your head.

Hitting is extremely dependent on the batter's mental state. If the batter comes to the plate with a positive outlook, if he mentally pictures little fielders with lots of green grass between them, he's probably going to get a hit. However, if you can make him see huge fielders wearing huge gloves with very little green grass between them, the batter is probably going to make an out. Your job, as a defensive pitcher, is to plug up the middle and take away the "green."

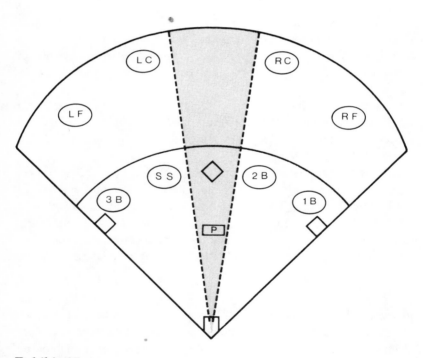

Exhibit 15:
There is no one in the gap directly behind the pitcher.

Backing Up

You will remember that the front of the pitching rubber is 46' away from the back point of home plate. As the pitcher steps towards the batter during the pitching motion and release, the actual distance between the pitcher and point of contact comes closer to 43'. At 43' you don't have much time to react to a ball hit up the middle. One of your objectives after releasing the ball should be to back up several steps, place yourself in a defensive position, and anticipate that the ball will be hit to you.

In the days of unlimited arc, the pitcher with a high arc had enough time to back up a significant distance. Some pitchers were able to back up towards the vicinity of 2nd base.

The 12' arc limits the distance you can back up because the drop time is not nearly as long. It does, however, give you enough time to back up 5 steps, or approximately 9'–10'. As shown in Exhibit 16, assuming you are using the One-Step Delivery, you have enough time to back up 4 steps and plant your left foot on the 5th step.

Specifically, your first step is forward with your left foot. The first step backward is also with your left foot (1). Then right (2), left (3), and right (4). The final step is not a full step back, but enough to bring the left foot (5) even with the right foot. Once your feet are positioned, get into whatever defensive position you normally use and prepare for a ball to be hit up the middle. You should be as prepared as any other infielder because, in reality, you have now become a 5th infielder.

If you are not in good physical shape, you can utilize a 3-Step Back Up instead of the 5-Step Back Up (exhibit 17). The same principle holds true, you are just two steps closer to the batter than with the 5-Step. Remember that every step back will give you more reaction time and make you a better defensive pitcher. Exhibit 18 shows the advantage of backing up. The farther you are away from the batter, the greater your reaction time and, therefore, the greater number of plays you will be able to make.

If you utilize the No-Step Delivery, you can save yourself one complete step and use a 4-Step Back Up. As shown in exhibit 19, since your left foot is already behind the pitching rubber, your first step back is with the right foot. Right (1), left (2), right (3), and bring the left foot (4) even with the right. You can see why experienced pitchers prefer the No-Step Delivery to the One-Step.

With the One Step Approach, and no back stepping, you assume your defensive position in front of the pitcher's plate, approximately 43' from home plate.

With the Five Step Back-Up, you assume your defensive position 9'-10' behind the pitcher's plate, or 55'-56' from home plate.

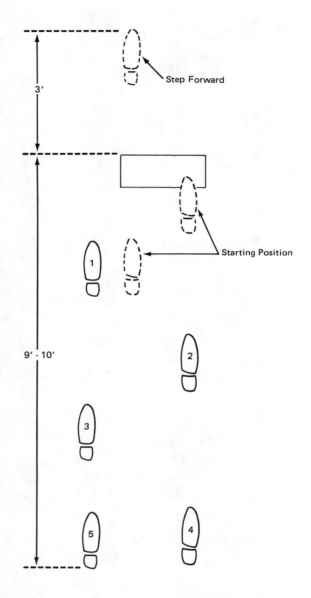

Exhibit 16:

5-Step back up. Your 1st step takes you 3' closer to the batter. Then you back up left (1), right (2), left (3), right (4), and plant your left foot (5) almost even with your right foot, ending up almost 10' behind the pitcher's plate.

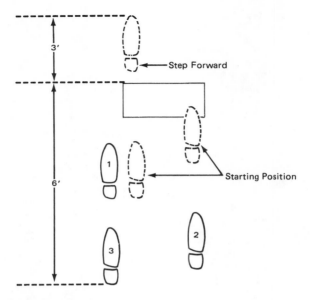

Exhibit 17:
3 Step back up. Similar to the 5 Step, except 2 full steps are eliminated.

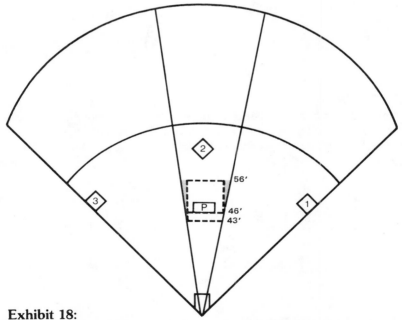

Exhibit 18:
You can cover significantly more ground at 56' than you can at 43'.

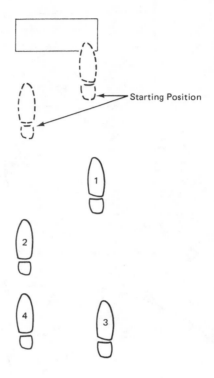

Exhibit 19:
With the No-Step delivery, your left foot is already behind the pitcher's plate. Therefore, the first step back is with the right foot (1). Then, left (2), right (3), and plant the left foot (4) almost even with the right.

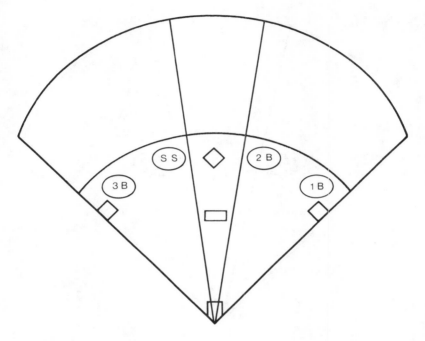

Exhibit 20:
The positioning of the infield with a weak fielding pitcher.

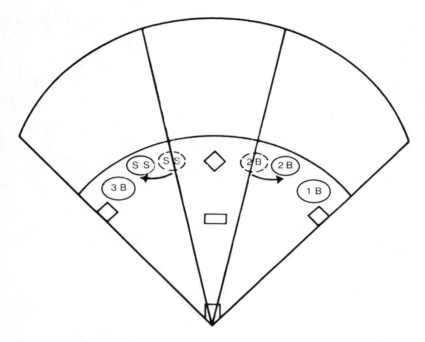

Exhibit 20A:
A good fielding pitcher allows'the shortstop and 2nd baseman to cheat a little, thereby reducing the gaps between SS-3B, and 1B-2B.

A further advantage of having a good defensive pitcher who can plug up the middle is that this will allow your shortstop and 2nd baseman to cheat a little more towards 3rd base or 1st base, thereby reducing the size of those gaps as well (exhibits 20 and 20A).

Large Gloves

Incredible as it may seem, I still see pitchers playing softball with baseball gloves. Some people still don't realize that baseball and softball are two different sports. Baseball gloves were designed to catch a baseball, not a 12″ softball. They are constructed with smaller fingers, a smaller pocket, and smaller webbing. They were not designed with softball in mind.

Too many players try to make the transition from baseball to softball without realizing they need a new glove. Softball gloves are not new. They were introduced years ago and have been specially designed for a 12″ softball.

Do you remember coaches telling you that you had to catch with two hands? Two hands were absolutely necessary years ago because gloves were significantly smaller and very poorly designed. Today's softball gloves are much larger. Although the "two hands" advice is still good advice, you see more players today making one handed catches. These players aren't hot dogs (generally); they simply have the appropriate glove and realize that two hands aren't always necessary.

A pitcher who uses a baseball glove is asking for trouble. He is closer to the batter and has less time to react to a batted ball than anyone else on the field. A softball glove is necessary simply in the interest of self preservation. But you should also want one from a defensive standpoint as well. A glove that is 4″ longer than your existing glove will allow you to cover 6% more area.

Don't believe me? Stand with your feet apart in a defensive position. Place a yard stick beginning mid-way between your left and right feet, extending your right. Leaving your pivot foot (right foot) stationary, move your left foot quickly to your right as if making a stab at a line drive to your right side. Measure the distance from the center of where you were standing to the end of your fingertips.

Now resume the original position, make a stab at an imaginary line drive to your left, and measure it. I measure a reach of approximately 63″ each way. A softball glove with a webbing 4″ longer than many older baseball gloves would extend the reach to about 67″, an increase of more than 6%.

I don't have to tell experienced softball players about the need for a large softball glove. They already know it. Cost? Around $75. Possibly more. But if you are going to keep it for 10 years, that averages out

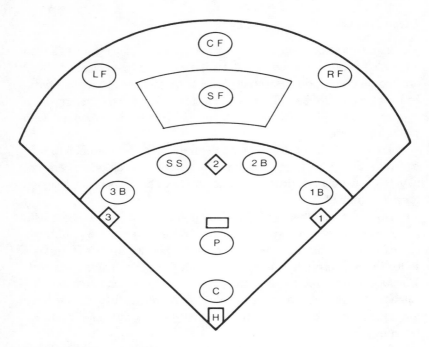

Exhibit 21:
Defensive arrangement with the traditional shortfielder playing between the center fielder and 2nd base.

to $7.50 per year. That's pretty cheap insurance considering that some batters come to the plate aiming at your head. Most people spend more than that each year renting bowling shoes.

Buy a good glove. The best you can afford. It will pay off in the long run.

Responsibility for Positioning of the Fielders

I firmly believe that it is the pitcher's responsibility to properly position the fielders, both infield and outfield. The pitcher is in the best position to determine what the batter's strengths and weaknesses are, and where the batter is most likely going to hit the ball. You should not pitch the ball until you are completely satisfied with the defensive

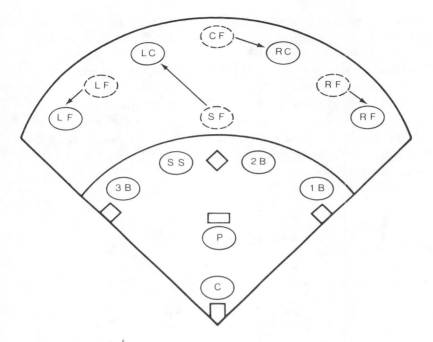

Exhibit 22:
4 across defensive arrangement. The short fielder moves to left-center field, the center fielder moves into right-center field and the left and right fielders move towards the foul lines.

arrangement. Any ball hit over the head of an outfielder is therefore your responsibility, not the outfielder's.

Defensive Arrangements

The generally accepted name for the 10th player in Slow Pitch is the Short Fielder. The early thinking was that the 10th defensive player could play the Short Field i.e., somewhere between the Infield and Outfield, with the primary purpose being to prevent short base hits up the middle (exhibit 21).

Although the original concept of the Short Fielder may have had some validity, thinking on this subject has changed. With the tremendous increase in the number of long ball hitters, relatively few teams use the Short Fielder today. Those teams that do are generally inexperienced teams playing in weak leagues.

Today the most commonly used defensive outfield arrangement is the 4-Across. Instead of playing with Outfielders in Left Field, Center Field, Right Field and with the Short Fielder positioned just behind 2nd base, as in Exhibit 21, most teams will opt for a Left Fielder, Left-Center Fielder, Right-Center Fielder, and Right Fielder, as in exhibit 22. Note that the Left Fielder and Right Fielder play closer to the lines, and there is no one positioned in dead center field.

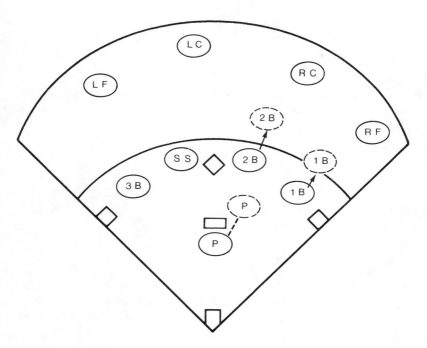

Exhibit 23:
Unusual defensive arrangement against a dead-pull left handed hitter.

From a pitcher's perspective, the advantage of this arrangement is that the size of the gaps between outfielders is reduced, reducing the chances of a ball going through the gap for a home run. Four straight singles against a 4-Across defense should yield only one or possibly two runs at the most, whereas a single home run could prove disastrous. And the odds of a team getting 4 straight hits are much less than a team getting one home run. Therefore, you should usually use the 4-Across Defense.

Other unusual defensive arrangements can be concocted if needed. One I have seen used against dead-pull left-handed hitters is to move the 2nd baseman well back onto the outfield grass and the 1st baseman also back several steps (exhibit 23).

After releasing the ball, the pitcher backsteps more towards the location of the 2nd baseman rather than directly back towards 2nd base.

The advantage of this arrangement is that it reduces the green available to the hitter on the right side of the field. It can also have a psychological impact on him when he sees that everyone on the field knows what he is going to do. Usually it forces him to try to go the opposite way, a swing he is usually very uncomfortable with.

The drawbacks are that a slow-rolling ground ball to 2nd base can turn into an infield hit, or a successful hit to the opposite field can turn into an extra base hit.

Just remember that, as the pitcher, you are better able to analyze a hitter's intentions than anyone else on the field. Watch him closely, position your defense according to the hitter, and pitch him smart.

In Summary

- The pitcher is closer to the batter and has less time to react than anyone else on the field.

- Assume that every batter is aiming at your head.

- A pitcher who can plug up the middle can allow his defense to cheat a little, thereby reducing the size of other gaps and holes.

- You should back up after every pitch, using either the 3-step, 4-step, or 5-step Back Up.

- Buy the best and largest legal softball glove you can afford.

- A larger softball glove can increase the defensive area you can cover by approximately 6%.,

- A pitcher should not pitch until the defense is where he wants it. A ball hit over an outfielder's head is the pitcher's responsibility, not the outfielder's.

Chapter 9

Umpires

Consistency. That's the most important thing to look for in an Umpire. Few Umpires totally agree on the strike zone. Each seems to have a slightly different perspective of a Slow Pitch strike but as long as the Umpire is <u>consistent</u> in what he calls balls and strikes, you have the capability to adjust to what he is calling.

Overall, there are three distinct types of Umpires.

The first type of Umpire is the one with a large strike zone. By large I mean he allows you to pitch to the extremes of the defined strike zone. Pitches that cut the corners are called strikes, pitches that reach the 12' legal arc are called strikes, low (but legal) pitches are strikes, deep pitches behind the plate are strikes. This Umpire allows the pitcher to work the batter. Batters who get behind in the count are forced to swing at close pitches to protect the plate. These Umpires respect the pitcher's ability and force the batter to swing at pitches that aren't necessarily the best.

Scores in these games are generally lower. Umpires like this are the best from the pitcher's perspective, but usually hard to find. You will find them frequently at higher levels of competition, rarely at lower levels of competition.

The second type of Umpire has a small strike zone. By that I mean he calls anything around the corners a ball. The entire ball must cross through the strike zone to be considered a strike. He wants the pitcher to groove the pitch so that the batter can rip the ball. He is a hitter's Umpire, believes that softballs are meant to be hit hard and far, and takes much of the strategy of pitching away.

Scores in these games are usually high with a lot of home runs, especially on a field with a fence. Personally, I don't care for these Umpires but, if they are consistent in their calls for both sides, you can't complain too much.

The third and worst kind of Umpire is the one who is inconsistent. One pitch he calls a strike. The next pitch in the exact same location he calls a ball. The strike zone changes with each batter, or each inning, or when the score shifts in favor of one team or the other. You can't adjust to that kind of Umpire because you don't know what to expect. These are the most frustrating type of Umpires for a pitcher.

How does a pitcher determine what an Umpire perceives as the strike zone? Three ways. First, ask the Umpire himself. Before the game simply introduce yourself to the Umpire and ask him his definition of the strike zone. How does he call the plate? Does he give a deep strike? Does he use the backstop as a guide for the 12' limit?

Most Umpires will be glad to discuss this with you. If you understand their strike zone, it makes their job easier.

You will be amazed at what you hear. I had one Umpire who took a bat, measured one bat's length behind the point of the plate, drew a line and said, "Anything between the plate and that line is a strike."

Technically correct? No. However, I had an advantage over the other pitcher who never asked. It took him several innings before he determined what the Umpire's strike zone was. We won the game.

The second way is to test the Umpire. In the early innings, test above the 12' limit and test the low, short pitch. If he calls either a strike, file it away for when you can use it to your advantage later in the game.

The third way to determine an Umpire's consistency is through experience. Tournaments and games away from home are a new experience because everything is totally different. However, in your local area there are only a limited number of Umpires and eventually you will start seeing the same ones repeatedly. Study the Umpire closely and remember his strike zone. Or, ask your teammates who may have seen him call a game before. What you learn before the game starts can give you a tremendous advantage over the other pitcher.

By and large, many Umpires the average Slow Pitch Pitcher will face are rather inexperienced in Slow Pitch. It is not uncommon for an Umpire to come to a Slow Pitch game directly from Umpiring a baseball or Fast Pitch game. Umpires are only human and it is just as tough for them to adjust to a different strike zone as it is for a batter.

Umpires are paid $10–$20 per game to take abuse from both sides for about two hours. No matter what decision, the Umpire loses and one side is mad. Fans only make the situation worse.

Sometimes I wonder what motivates an Umpire to become an Umpire. Money is only a part of it because they usually are underpaid.

I've come to the conclusion that it is either a love of the game or a lack of common sense. Either way, we still need them to play the game.

In Summary

- Umpires have different perceptions of the Slow Pitch strike zone.

- Regardless of his perception of the strike zone, the best Umpire is one who is consistent. The worst Umpire is the one who is inconsistent.

- Complaining about an Umpire's strike zone does you no good. It is <u>imperative</u> that you determine the Umpire's strike zone in the early innings and <u>adjust</u> to it accordingly.

- Test the limits of the Umpire's strike zone. It only costs you a ball to learn what may be a potentially important piece of information.

- Talk to the Umpire before the game. Most are friendly and are happy to discuss things with you.

- Umpires are generally underpaid for the amount of verbal abuse they take.

- If you ever feel like getting all over an Umpire's case, stop and think about the last time that an Umpire failed to show up at one of your games. If you really want to play a competitive game, <u>any</u> impartial Umpire is better than none at all.

Chapter 10

Miscellaneous Topics

This chapter is a compilation of miscellaneous thoughts, theories, and strategies that don't really fit logically anywhere else in the book. Rather than omit them, I'll simply throw them into this last chapter. I hope you find them helpful.

Using the Softball to your Advantage

Most average leagues with a limited budget require the home team to supply one new ball for each game. In the event that a foul ball is hit out of play, the back-up ball usually becomes the best practice ball available from either team's ball bag and has probably already seen a lot of action.

Any experienced pitcher knows that the more a ball is used, the deader it becomes and the shorter distance it will travel. You can see a significant difference between a new ball and a practice ball.

There is also a significant difference between the liveliness of a ball in the first inning vs. the seventh inning. Don't forget this. There are some long ball hitters you can never keep in the park regardless of which ball you use, or which inning it is. But you would be surprised at the number of marginal home run hitters who might be able to hit a home run in the first inning, but not in the seventh inning.

O.K. It's the first inning, man on second base, two out. Clean-up hitter at bat. How do you get the lively ball out of the game? It's not easy but it can be done occasionally. The trick is to force him to hit a long foul ball. On the first pitch, jam him. Pitch him inside. A pitch that is tempting, but not too good. If you are lucky enough to get him to hit a long foul ball, <u>let it go</u>. Tell your outfielder to let it go. "To speed up the play," get the back-up ball from the Umpire and let the other team retrieve the new ball. Result: the deader ball is in the game. When the new ball is retrieved and thrown to you while you are holding the older ball, throw the <u>new</u> ball back to the umpire and keep the old one in the game. If the other team complains, too bad. Nothing in the rules states that you have to pitch the newer ball. Only the Umpire can return the new ball into the game.

Of course, when your team comes up to bat with the old ball in the game, ask the Umpire for a new ball. If he refuses, have your first batter hit a long foul ball to get the new ball back into the game.

Intentional Walks

Sometimes you are going to face hitters who can do it all: good power, good placement, can hit a single, can hit the gaps, and there is not much you can do to stop them. In certain circumstances you do have one option you can use to stop these hitters and that is the Intentional Walk. There are actually two different types of Intentional Walks of which you should be aware.

Unlike baseball where four pitches must be thrown outside the strike zone in order to walk a batter, Slow Pitch softball allows you to simply point to first base and tell the Umpire that you want to walk the batter. No pitches are required. This is allowed to speed up the game. And, this is the situation most commonly used when you just don't want to pitch to a batter.

When would you want to utilize this? As an obvious example, assume that late in the game you are up by a run, one out, runners on second and third with a long ball hitter up. A long pop fly ties the game; a single or gapper wins it. A logical move would be to walk the power hitter intentionally to load up the bases, and pitch the next batter low, looking for a ground ball and a double play. It may backfire but, unless you have the power hitter's number, it may be the lesser of two evils.

There is another use of this form of Intentional Walk. Occasionally you may be facing a hitter who will kill you. No matter what you do, no matter how you pitch him, he can hit you somewhere. One way to deal with him is to take the bat out of his hands in successive at bats early in the game. As long as it doesn't hurt you, put him on. Don't even let him swing the bat. The strategy is that if he doesn't swing the bat in the early innings, he will be cold when you finally let him swing late in the game. Hopefully his timing will be off just enough, and that he will be so mad or frustrated, that on his first swing he will hit the ball off center for an out. It doesn't always work, but . . . sometimes.

The second type of Intentional Walk is when you purposely throw four pitches outside the strike zone. With some hitters you know, either from past experience or you can see it in their eyes, there is no way they are going to take a walk. They are there to swing the bat.

With a batter like this, under no circumstances should you give him a good pitch to swing at. Throw a short pitch, a deep pitch, whatever. Make him swing at a ball. Individuals like this are not smart ballplayers. They rarely take a walk and most of the time you can get them to swing at a bad pitch.

Weather Conditions

One thing most pitchers don't take into consideration is the weather on the day of the game. Have you ever noticed how a ball travels farther on some days than others? How it usually seems to travel 15'–30' farther on a hot, dry, sunny day than it does on cold or cool damp days, or very humid days.

The distance the ball travels on any given day seems to have something to do with the density of the air. I'm not a scientific individual and can't give you a scientific kind of explanation for it, but it is true.

Air density can come into play when you are playing on a fence field against a team of marginal home run hitters. By marginal I mean that on any given day some of them may be able to put the ball over the fence, but not consistently.

A pitcher can use this to his advantage. Once a hitter puts a ball over a fence, he generally thinks he can do it every time up. He doesn't think about the type of ball, the time of game, how hard or soft the ball has become, or what the weather was like the last time he hit the home run. He just sees the fence.

On certain days you can use this to your advantage. On days when the ball is traveling well, don't challenge the marginal home run hitter too much, especially in the early innings when the ball is still hard and lively. Perhaps in the later innings but not early in the game.

On days when the ball is not traveling well, challenge this hitter. Let him go for the fence. Chances are he won't hurt you and he will only hit a long pop fly.

Obviously the same holds true when you are playing in the rain, in night games, early morning games where the ball picks up the morning dew, or the like. Remember that this only applies to marginal home run hitters. There are many players who are not impacted by the weather. With 275' fences, you can throw them a croquet ball and they'll still hit it over.

Changing Pitchers

Most competitive teams have several pitchers on their roster. Some teams use a regular rotation between the pitchers, while other teams utilize certain pitchers as starters and others as relievers.

In baseball and Fast Pitch, the primary reason a relief pitcher is needed is because the starting pitcher becomes tired. He loses some of his speed, he begins missing his target, and the batters start teeing off on him.

In Slow Pitch, rarely does a pitcher become tired (unless we're talking about pitching in a tournament, but that's another story). There is no speed on the pitch so he can't lose it.

Rather, the usual problem in Slow Pitch is that the batters begin zeroing in on the pitcher's rhythm. It may take four, five, or six innings but eventually the batters will get your rhythm down and begin hammering you. Base hit after base hit.

As soon as it becomes evident that the batters have your number, expect your coach to change pitchers. Three out of four times all it takes to break a rally is a new pitcher with a different delivery, different motion, different arc, and different spin. A new pitcher will usually throw the batter's timing off by just a split second, enough for the batter to miss-hit and end the rally.

As soon as the relief pitcher starts getting hit around, your coach will probably change pitchers again. Anything to throw the batter's timing off.

Ways to Throw Off a Batter's Timing

As we have said time and again, timing is the key to successful hitting. A successful pitcher is one who can throw off a batter's timing.

The following is a brief summary of ways you can throw a batter's timing off. Some are obvious, others are not.

- vary the arc
- vary the spin
- vary the location
- vary the length of backswing
- vary the type of delivery
- vary the time between pitches

- quick pitch

- confer with the catcher, coach, or some infielder to delay and make the batter wait

- change pitchers

- make a great defensive play or turn a key double play, thereby demoralizing the batter and the opposing team

Checklist of Some Situations to be Considered Before Pitching

Up to this point we have been primarily talking about how to get a specific batter out. Just as important as analyzing the batter is analyzing the game situation. Different game situations call for different pitching strategies.

The following checklist covers some of the things you should consider.

GAME SITUATIONS TO BE CONSIDERED BEFORE PITCHING

General
1 Is a pop fly needed or to be prevented?
2 Is a ground ball needed for a double play?
3 Should the ball be kept from being hit behind the runner?
4 Who are the most reliable fielders in tight situations?
5 What is the batter's position in the line-up?
6 What has the batter done in previous times at bat?
7 Are any other special measures called for?
8 Are all defensive men aware of the situation?

No runners on base
1 Pitch to the batter.
2 Exploit his batting weaknesses.

Runner on first base
1 Generally pitch short, especially with less than two outs.

Runner on second base
1 Pitch short and inside to a right hand batter, and short and outside to a left hand batter; keep the ball on the ground on the left side of the infield to keep the runner from advancing.

Runner on third base, less than two out
1 Unless the batter has some highly visible weaknesses, throw no deep pitches; usually keep the ball short and inside.

Runners on first and second
1 Always pitch short to get ground balls.

Your first pitch should usually be a strike. The exception should be when the batter typically swings at the first pitch, or to avoid establishing a pitching pattern.

In Summary

- A ball will travel farther in the early innings of a game.

- When it is to your advantage, get the lively ball out of the game.

- There are two forms of Intentional Walks, each of which can be used to your advantage.

- The ball will travel farther on some days than others, depending on the weather conditions.

- As soon as it becomes evident that batters have zeroed in on a pitcher's timing, change pitchers.

- There are many ways to throw a batter's timing off. Use them to your advantage.

- Always consider the game situation before pitching to any batter.

Appendix

This section contains those sections of the 1987 ASA Official Guide and Rule Book which are most applicable to pitching. I would strongly suggest that you read them several times, study them, and remember them.

A complete copy of the current ASA Official Guide can be obtained by writing to the ASA directly:

Amateur Softball Association
2801 N.E. 50th Street
Oklahoma City, OK 73111

The cost for the 1987 Official Guide was $2.50 plus shipping, a very inexpensive investment.

RULE 1, SECTION 58

Sec. 58. THE STRIKE ZONE. (SP ONLY) The strike zone is that space over any part of home plate between the batter's highest shoulder and his knees when the batter assumes a natural batting stance.

RULE 3, SECTION 3

Sec. 3. THE OFFICIAL SOFTBALL.

a. Shall be a regular, smooth-seamed, concealed stitched or flat surfaced ball.
b. Shall have a center core made of either No. 1 quality, long fibre kapok, a mixture of cork and rubber, a polyurethane mixture or other materials approved by the A.S.A.
c. May be hand or machine wound, with a fine quality twisted yarn, and covered with latex or rubber cement.
d. Shall have a cover cemented to the ball by application of cement to the underside of the cover, and sewn with waxed thread of cotton or linen, or shall have a molded cover bonded to the core with an authentic facsimile of stitching as approved by the ASA.
e. Shall have a cover of chrome tanned top grain horsehide or cowhide; synthetic material; or made of other materials approved by the A.S.A.
f. The 12-inch (30.0 cm) ball shall be between 11-⅞ inches (30.0 cm) and 12-⅛ inches (31.0 cm) in circumference, and shall weigh between 6¼ ounces (180.0 g) and 7 ounces (200.0 g). The smooth-seam style shall not have less than 88 stitches in each cover, sewn by the two-needle method, or with an authentic facsimile of stitching as approved by the ASA.
g. The 11-inch (27.0 cm) ball shall be between 10-⅞ inches (27.0 cm) and 11-⅛ inches (28.0 cm) in circumference, and shall weigh between 5-⅞ ounces (165.0 g) and 6-⅛ ounces (175.0 g). The smooth-seam style shall not have less than 80 stitches in each cover, sewn by the two-needle method, or with an authentic facsimile of stitching as approved by the ASA.
h. The white-stitch 12 inch ball shall be used in the following ASA championship play: Men's and Women's fast pitch, Boys' Junior Olympic Fast Pitch and Slow Pitch and Girls' Junior Olympic Fast Pitch. Beginning in 1989 it must have a COR of .50 or under and be so marked.
i. The red-stitch 12 inch ball with a COR of .47 and under shall be used in all adult men's slow pitch and Co-Ed slow pitch, and must have a marking of MSP-47.
j. The red-stitch 11 inch ball with a COR of .47 and under shall be used in the following ASA Play: Women's Slow Pitch and all Girls' Junior Olympic Slow Pitch. It must have a GWSP-47 marking.
k. Softballs used in A.S.A. championship tournament play must meet standards set by the A.S.A. Equipment Standards Committee as shown below, and must be stamped with the ASA logo.

THE OFFICIAL SOFTBALL SPECIFICATIONS ARE AS FOLLOWS:

SOFTBALL	THREAD COLOR	MINIMUM SIZE	MAXIMUM SIZE	MINIMUM SIZE	MAXIMUM SIZE	MARKING
12-inch FP (30.0 cm)	white	11 ⅞ in 30.0 cm	12 ⅛ in 31.0 cm	6¼ oz 180.0 g	7 oz 200.0 g	A.S.A. LOGO
12-inch SP (30.0 cm)	red	11 ⅞ in 30.0 cm	12 ⅛ in 31.0 cm	6¼ oz 180.0 g	7 oz 200.0 g	MSP-47

RULE 6, PITCHING REGULATIONS (SLOW PITCH)

Sec. 1. THE PITCHER SHALL TAKE A POSITION WITH BOTH FEET FIRMLY ON THE GROUND AND WITH ONE OR BOTH FEET IN CONTACT WITH, BUT NOT OFF THE SIDE OF, THE PITCHER'S PLATE. While the pivot foot is in contact with the pitcher's plate and throughout the delivery, both the pivot and non-pivot foot must be within the length of the pitcher's plate when on the ground or on the pitcher's plate.

a. *Preliminary to pitching, the pitcher must come to a full and complete stop, with the ball in front of the body. The front of the body must face the batter.*
b. This position must be maintained at least one second and not more than 10 seconds before starting the delivery.

c. The pitcher shall not be considered in pitching position unless the catcher is in position to receive the pitch.

NOTE: To indicate to the pitcher that he may not start the pitch, the umpire should raise one hand with the palm facing the pitcher. "NO PITCH" shall be declared if the pitcher pitches while the umpire has his hand in said position.

▶**Sec. 2. THE PITCH** starts when the pitcher makes any motion that is part of his windup after the required pause. Prior to the required pause, any windup may be used. The pivot foot must remain in contact with the pitcher's plate until the pitched ball leaves the hand. *If a step is taken, it can be forward or BACKWARD, provided the foot is in contact with the pitching plate when the ball is released and the step is within the 24 inches (60.96cm) of the pitcher's plate and simultaneous with the release of the ball.*

PLAY — F1 has both feet on the rubber. F1 removes one foot by stepping backward and then pitches ball to B1. B1 does not swing at the pitch. RULING — Legal pitch. A step with the free foot is not required in slow pitch, but if one is taken, it can be forward or backward as long as the pivot foot remains in contact with the pitching plate until the ball is released.

Sec. 3. A LEGAL DELIVERY SHALL BE A BALL WHICH IS DELIVERED TO THE BATTER WITH AN UNDERHANDED MOTION.

PLAY (1) — The pitcher comes to a two-second stop, takes the ball in his pitching hand over the top of his head, down and around in a windmill type action, and releases the ball the first time past the hip. RULING — Legal. A windmill delivery is legal if the ball is released the first time past the hip and all other aspects of the pitching rule are followed.

PLAY (2) — The pitcher releases the ball during a pitch with his palm on top of the ball and with the ball facing the ground. RULING — Legal.

a. The pitch shall be released at a moderate speed. The speed is left entirely up to the umpire. The umpire shall warn the pitcher who delivers a pitch with excessive speed. If the pitcher repeats such an act after being warned, he shall be removed from the pitcher's position for the remainder of the game.

PLAY — After one warning, F1 again delivers a pitch with excessive speed. Plate umpire orders that F1 must be removed from the game. Manager attempts to change F1 to an outfield position but umpire rules that the pitcher cannot participate in any position for the remainder of the game. RULING — Illegal. F1 shall be removed from the pitching position for the remainder of the game but may participate in the game in any other position.

b. The hand shall be below the hip.
c. The ball must be delivered with a perceptible arc, and reach a height of at least six feet (1.83m) from the ground while not exceeding a maximum height of 12 feet (3.66m) from the ground.

PLAY — Pitcher releases ball in a pitch to the batter and the ball reaches a height of 15 feet before beginning its downward flight toward the plate. RULING — Illegal Pitch.

d. The catcher must be within the lines of the catcher's box until the pitched ball is batted or reaches the catcher's box.
e. The catcher shall return the ball directly to the pitcher after each pitch, except after a strikeout or putout made by the catcher.
f. The pitcher has 20 seconds to release the next pitch after receiving the ball from the catcher.

EFFECT — Sec. 3e: An additional "ball" is awarded to the batter.

PLAY —   R1 on first base. Count on batter is one strike and no balls. Batter hits a foul
ball which the catcher retrieves and gives the ball to the umpire. The umpire
gives the catcher a new ball which he throws to the first baseman. RULING
— A ball is awarded to the batter. In slow pitch, the rule applies regardless of
whether or not runners were on base.

Sec. 4. THE PITCHER MAY USE ANY WINDUP DESIRED, PROVIDING:

a.   He does not make any motion to pitch without immediately delivering the ball to the
batter.
b.   His windup is a continuous motion.
c.   He does not use a windup in which there is a stop or reversal of the pitching motion.
d.   He delivers the ball toward home plate on the first forward swing of the pitching arm
past the hip.
e.   He does not continue to wind up after he releases the ball.
f.   He does not pitch the ball behind his back or between his legs.

Sec. 5. THE PITCHER SHALL NOT DELIBERATELY DROP, ROLL OR BOUNCE THE BALL WHILE IN THE PITCHING POSITION IN ORDER TO PREVENT THE BATTER FROM STRIKING IT.

Sec. 6. THE PITCHER SHALL NOT, AT ANY TIME DURING THE GAME, BE ALLOWED TO USE TAPE OR ANY OTHER FOREIGN SUBSTANCE UPON THE BALL, THE PITCHING HAND OR FINGERS, NOR SHALL ANY OTHER PLAYER APPLY A FOREIGN SUBSTANCE TO THE BALL. Under the supervision and control of the umpire, powdered resin may be used to dry the hands. The pitcher shall not wear a sweatband, bracelet or similar type item on the wrist or forearm of the pitching arm.

PLAY (1) — Pitcher with tape on pitching hand. RULING — Illegal. Must remove tape or
be replaced.

PLAY (2) — The pitcher holding the ball in his glove hand, delivers the pitch from the
glove hand. RULING — Illegal pitch. He must deliver the ball with his bare
hand.

Sec. 7. AT THE BEGINNING OF EACH HALF INNING OR WHEN A PITCHER RELIEVES ANOTHER, NOT MORE THAN ONE MINUTE MAY BE USED TO DELIVER NOT MORE THAN FIVE PITCHES TO THE CATCHER OR OTHER TEAMMATE. Play shall be suspended during this time. For excessive warm-up pitches, a pitcher shall be penalized by awarding a ball to the batter for each pitch in excess of five.

Sec. 8. THE PITCHER SHALL NOT ATTEMPT A QUICK RETURN OF THE BALL BEFORE THE BATTER HAS TAKEN HIS POSITION OR IS OFF BALANCE AS A RESULT OF A PREVIOUS PITCH.

►NOTE: It is an illegal pitch if a fielder takes up a position in the batter's line of vision or,
with deliberate unsportsmanlike intent, act in a manner to distract the batter. A
pitch does not have to be released. The offended player shall be ejected from
the game and an illegal pitch shall be declared.

EFFECT — Sec. 1-8: Any infraction of Sections 1-8 is an illegal pitch. A ball shall be called
on the batter. Baserunners are not advanced.
EXCEPTION: If a batter strikes at any illegal pitch, it shall be a strike and there shall be no
penalty for such an illegal pitch. The ball shall remain in play if hit by the batter. If an illegal
pitch is called during an appeal play, the appeal is cancelled.

NOTE: An illegal pitch shall be called immediately when it becomes illegal. If called by
the plate umpire, it shall be called in a voice so that the catcher and the batter
will hear it. The plate umpire will also give the delayed dead ball signal. If called
by the base umpire, it shall be called so that the nearest fielder shall hear it. The
base umpire shall also give the delayed dead ball signal. Failure of players to
hear the call shall not void the call.

Sec. 9. NO PITCH SHALL BE DECLARED WHEN:

a. The pitcher pitches during the suspension of play.
b. The runner is called out for leaving the base before the pitched ball reaches home plate.
c. The pitcher pitches before the baserunner has retouched his base after a foul ball has been declared and the ball is dead.
d. THE BALL SLIPS FROM THE PITCHER'S HAND DURING HIS WINDUP OR DURING THE BACKSWING.

EFFECT — Sec. 9a-d: The ball is dead and all subsequent action on that pitch is cancelled.

e. NO PLAYER, MANAGER OR COACH SHALL CALL "TIME," EMPLOY ANY OTHER WORD OR PHRASE, OR COMMIT ANY ACT WHILE THE BALL IS ALIVE AND IN PLAY FOR THE OBVIOUS PURPOSE OF TRYING TO MAKE THE PITCHER COMMIT AN ILLEGAL PITCH.

EFFECT — Sec. 9e: No pitch shall be declared and a warning issued to the offending team. A repeat of this type of act by the team warned shall result in the offender being removed from the game.

PLAY — REFER TO RULE 6, SECTION 9e EFFECT (FAST PITCH).

Sec. 10. THERE SHALL BE ONLY ONE CHARGED CONFERENCE BETWEEN THE MANAGER OR OTHER TEAM REPRESENTATIVE FROM THE DUGOUT WITH EACH AND EVERY PITCHER IN AN INNING. The second charged conference shall result in the removal of the pitcher from the pitching position for the remainder of the game.

RULE 7, SECTION 6

Sec. 6. A STRIKE IS CALLED BY THE UMPIRE:

a. (SP ONLY) For each legally pitched ball entering the strike zone before touching the ground and at which the batter does not swing. It is not a strike if the pitched ball touches home plate and is not swung at.

EFFECT — Sec. 6a: (SP ONLY) The ball is dead.

b. (SP ONLY) For each pitched ball struck at and missed by the batter.

EFFECT — Sec. 6b: (SP ONLY) The ball is dead.

c. For each foul tip held by the catcher.

EFFECT — Sec. 6c: (SP ONLY) The batter is out if it is the third strike. The ball is dead on any strike.

d. (SP ONLY) For each foul ball not legally caught, including the third strike.
e. For each pitched ball struck at and misses which touches any part of the batter.

PLAY — On third strike, B3 strikes at and missed a pitch. Ball strikes his arm or person.
RULING — B3 is out. Ball becomes dead.

f. When any part of the batter's person is hit with his own batted ball when he is in the batter's box and he has less than two strikes.
g. When a delivered ball by the pitcher hits the batter while the ball is in the strike zone.

EFFECT — Sec. 6d-g: The ball is dead and baserunners must return to their bases without liability to be put out.

RULE 7, SECTION 7

Sec. 7. A BALL IS CALLED BY THE UMPIRE:

a. For each legally pitched ball which does not enter the strike zone, touches the ground before reaching home plate, or touches home plate and at which the batter does not swing.

EFFECT — Sec. 7a: (SP ONLY) The ball is dead. Baserunners may not advance.

b. (SP ONLY) For each illegally pitched ball.

EFFECT — Sec. 7b: (SP ONLY) The ball is dead. Baserunners may not advance. EXCEPTION: If the batter swings at the illegal pitch, the illegal pitch is ignored.

c. (SP ONLY) When a delivered ball by the pitcher hits the batsman outside of the strike zone.
d. When the catcher fails to return the ball directly to the pitcher as required in Rule 6, Section 3e.
e. When the pitcher fails to pitch the ball within 20 seconds.
f. For each excessive warm-up pitch.

EFFECT — Sec. 7c-f: The ball is dead. Baserunners may not advance.

Notes

Notes